THE
EXPLORERS

**A STORY OF FEARLESS OUTCASTS,
BLUNDERING GENIUSES, AND
IMPOSSIBLE SUCCESS**

MARTIN DUGARD

SIMON & SCHUSTER

NEW YORK   LONDON   TORONTO   SYDNEY   NEW DELHI

90

Simon & Schuster
1230 Avenue of the Americas
New York, NY 10020

First Simon & Schuster hardcover edition June 2014

SIMON & SCHUSTER and colophon are registered trademarks of Simon & Schuster, Inc.

For information about special discounts for bulk purchases, please contact Simon & Schuster Special Sales at 1-866-506-1949 or business@simonandschuster.com.

The Simon & Schuster Speakers Bureau can bring authors to your live event. For more information or to book an event, contact the Simon & Schuster Speakers Bureau at 1-866-248-3049 or visit our website at www.simonspeakers.com.

Interior design by Ruth Lee-Mui

Manufactured in the United States of America

10 9 8 7 6 5 4 3 2 1

Library of Congress Cataloging-in-Publication Data

Dugard, Martin.
   The explorers : a story of fearless outcasts, blundering geniuses, and impossible success / Martin Dugard.
      pages   cm
   Includes bibliographical references and index.
1. Explorers—Biography.   I. Title.
   G200.D84 2014
   910.92'2—dc23   2013040158
ISBN 978-1-4516-7757-7
ISBN 978-1-4516-7759-1 (ebook)

For Callie

"We rejoice in our sufferings, knowing that suffering produces endurance, endurance produces character, and character produces hope. And hope does not disappoint us."

Romans 5:3–5

CONTENTS

ix

CONTENTS

THE
EXPLORERS

PROLOGUE

Soon it will be over.

John Hanning Speke has waited five years for the verdict. Now, on the eve of the great debate that will decide the outcome, he stalks through the dying grass of his uncle's estate in soft, precise steps. A Lancaster breechloader shotgun is cradled in the crook of his right arm. The left barrel is cocked and ready to shoot. George's man beats the brush out front, doing his best, but having an unlucky day scaring up partridge. The ancient Romans used to call such men "explorers," from the Latin *explorare*—"to cry out." But the definition has changed. No longer does it only apply to men who wander ahead in the fields and flush game. Now it also defines those adventurers who travel deep into undiscovered lands, then return to civilization to tell others what they saw.

Which is why, on this day, Daniel Davis is more commonly known as a groundskeeper, while John Hanning Speke is famous around the world as an explorer.

George Fuller himself, Speke's cousin, walks sixty yards to his right. This way their fields of fire don't overlap. Not that it matters—Speke and Fuller have pulled the trigger twice in the past two hours, hitting nothing at all.

Speke is unbothered by their failure. Killing small birds is not why he insisted on a few hours in the fields before dinner. The hunt is Speke's escape. Before he was an explorer, before Burton and the Nile, and before the public accusations that made his life a living hell, he was a hunter. He stalked and killed beasts of all sizes and ferocity, in Europe and Asia and Africa. His prowess is so renowned that a rare species of gazelle was named in his honor—a species that he personally discovered and then promptly shot. The hunt is where his nerves grow calm and insecurities cannot intrude. Everything is simple on the hunt, just like Speke. The fancy words and well-crafted arguments of a hedonist intellectual like Richard Francis Burton have no place.

Today, of all days, as Speke's mind races and he tries to arrange his words for that moment tomorrow morning when he will gingerly step up onto the speaker's platform before a crowd that will be no less ferocious than a lion in the wild, he desperately needs the clarity and calm of the hunt.

The field here at Neston Park, as the Fuller family estate is known, is separated from another by a two-foot-high stone wall. The young aristocrat can easily step over with the shotgun in his hand, but he chooses to wedge the butt in the rocks, so that the barrels point to the sky.

Tomorrow Speke will travel to Bath and debate Richard Francis Burton in the great auditorium. The newspapers are calling it the Nile Debate. Tickets are sold out. Thousands are taking the train from London to decide for themselves which man discovered the source of the Nile River, solving a geographical mystery that has perplexed mankind since the ancient Egyptians.

The winner will be known throughout history for the achievement. He will be wealthy and famous, and a legend in his own time—if not forever.

The loser will be disgraced and considered a fraud, his every accomplishment subject to newfound scrutiny.

It will all come down to how each man presents his argument. This is where Speke is at a disadvantage. Never mind that he has traveled into deepest Africa on three occasions, risking his life in the name of exploration. Or that his travels have been more epic, and have revealed far more about the unknown world, than Burton's. No one in the audience will care about anything but the Nile, and which of them persuades them that he is the very special man who found that hole in the ground from which it springs.

Speke is an anxious, celibate loner. Burton is a black-eyed, priapic genius for whom exploration is secondary to learning obscure languages and having sex with native women. Speke knows that Burton will try to ruin him; that the former friend with the scars across both cheeks will stop at nothing to humiliate, to embarrass, and to destroy.

But he feels powerless to stop him. Speke's stumbling public speaking and limited intellectual capacity pale in comparison to Burton's dazzling oratory.

It is not hard for Speke to imagine the golden words that will spill forth from Burton's lips tomorrow, convincing one and all in rational, thoughtful sentences, planting great seeds of doubt about Speke's theories.

Those seeds will be followed by whispers of derision from the audience, building to scorn and perhaps even laughter as the debate progresses. Speke knows it. Burton, who already awaits him in Bath, knows it. All of England knows it, thanks to the newspapers making much of the Nile duel. The thought is almost too much to bear.

The Lancaster has no safety. Speke feels the shotgun muzzle push against his breast as he straddles the stone wall. He puts his hand atop the smooth rocks to brace himself, even as the weight of his body presses down hard on the twenty-eight-inch Damascus steel barrels.

He has no choice. No choice at all.

The air smells like rain. Dusk is falling.

Meanwhile, in Bath, Burton awaits.

THE SEVEN

A half million or so years ago, depending upon the latest anthropological theories, the fertile forest hunting grounds of central Africa began to feel overcrowded to its human population. The actual date doesn't matter. What's important is that one day, very long in the past, a traveler—alone, most likely—began marching north and east from the lush Olduvai Gorge, just to see what was over the horizon. When he liked what he saw, he kept going. The lone figure was an unconventional sort, or he would have been quite content to remain home with his tribe. He was probably more bored than bold; or maybe just hungry, in search of game. He didn't know how far he would travel, or if he would return once he grew homesick or scared.

In his mind, he was off for a long walk, nothing more. But it *was* something more—something far more—for that adventurous stroll constituted the first journey of exploration.

And that lone man was the world's first explorer.*

Encouraged by their friend's success, a handful of his tribe's more daring members took a peek over the horizon, too. Liking what they saw, they also kept going. Over the course of thousands of years, countless more joined the migration. We know that they reached modern-day Ethiopia at least 197,000 years ago, and modern Israel by 25,000 BC. Their descendants traveled into Europe, across Asia, through Siberia, and over a land bridge into the Americas. In time they invented numbers and alphabets, built great cities, painted magnificent works of art, and sailed the seas in mighty vessels handcrafted for just that purpose. They kept on sailing until the oceans had been charted. Then they stepped back onto land and wandered across all they had not seen before, until there was no horizon over which mankind had not peered.

In London, a diagonal mile through Kensington Gardens

---

*Referring back to the etymology of the word "explorer," another noteworthy example of how a word changes can be seen in the word "Roger." Now used primarily as a common name, it was once more associated with the act of sexual congress. The dread pirates of the Caribbean, for instance, did not sail the flag of the Jolly Roger because they were happy guys named Roger. It should also be noted that the term Roger, in some parts of the world, is still slang for sex. Based on all this, one can easily imagine that at some point two or three centuries down the road there will be children with the endearing name of "Fucker."

from the Speke obelisk, rises Lowther Lodge, the headquarters of the Royal Geographical Society. The RGS, as it is known by its membership, has been the unofficial sanctioning body of global exploration for almost two centuries. The lodge is a tall brick building constructed in the style of Queen Anne architecture, with gable roofs, five lofty chimneys, and a fleet of mud-spattered Range Rovers in the gravel parking lot. Granite statues of David Livingstone and Ernest Shackleton hover in the second-story alcoves overlooking the sidewalks of Kensington Gore, as if urging the shoppers en route to Harrod's department store to seek a somewhat more adventurous calling.

Inside, the great rooms are drafty, the unpolished floorboards creak, and almost every bookshelf could use a good dusting. But some of history's most intoxicating discussions about exploration have taken place within those walls: Shackleton lectured about his famous open-boat journey across the Southern Ocean; Robert Falcon Scott discussed his upcoming (and, eventually, ill-fated) race to the South Pole; Sir Edmund Hillary briefed the Society upon his return from Everest, and Neil Armstrong spoke about becoming the first man to set foot on the moon. When David Livingstone's mummified body was returned from Africa, it was displayed in the RGS map room before being borne to Westminster Abbey for burial.* Thousands filed through to pay their respects. To add

---

*At the time, the RGS headquarters was at 1 Savile Row. This is now the home of the tailor firm Gieves & Hawkes. A photo of Livingstone's coffin is still on display in the location of the former map room.

the feeling of a proper African jungle, the fellows arranged for a thicket of potted palm trees to be placed along the walls.

Upstairs in the attic, the Society's archives contain the original letters of explorers who charted Asia, Africa, North America, South America, and Australia in the eighteenth and nineteenth centuries. Out back, in a glass structure that looks and feels very much like I. M. Pei's pyramid at the Louvre, are more of exploration's greatest relics: rare rocks, clothing, journals, letters, and the first maps of new lands, hand-drawn by the explorers themselves.

The most coveted item at the RGS, however, is a simple award bestowed every year (except during wartime) since 1831, when King William IV of Britain offered an annual gift of 50 guineas to encourage discovery. In 1839, rather than merely giving a cash prize, the RGS minted a gold medal of equal value for the winner. The men and women who have won that award read like a who's who of exploration: Ross, Franklin, Scott, Peary, Fremont, Stanley, Lindbergh, and on.

A proclamation accompanies each medal, citing the discoverer's great accomplishment. Captain Sir John Ross in 1834, for instance, was praised "for his discovery of Boothia Felix and King William Land and for his famous sojourn of four winters in the Arctic." Thomas Simpson, when receiving the first gold medal in 1839, was given the award "for tracing the hitherto unexplored coast of North America."

These are achievements that stir the soul, fire the imagination, and (in the case of Ross and his four polar winters) cause a subconscious shiver at the mere thought of the hardship endured. More than simple journeys, the gold medal adventures were ordeals in the loftiest sense of the word. Left unsaid in the proclamations were words like "frostbite" and "starvation" and "suffered the death of his comrades," which were just as much a part of an endeavor as the eventual accomplishment—in fact, more so. Joshua Slocum, the first man to sail alone around the world, fought four continuous days of storm as he exited the Strait of Magellan. African explorer Mungo Park walked until he nearly dropped dead from thirst. Shackleton went almost sixteen days without sleep during his open-boat journey. His clothes, constantly drenched from sea spray, froze each night.

This is how Apsley Cherry-Garrard described a five-week Antarctic expedition he and two men undertook in 1911. "The horror of the nineteen days it took us to travel from Cape Evans to Cape Crozier would have to be re-experienced to be appreciated. And anyone would be a fool who went again. It is not possible to describe it. It was the darkness that did it. I don't believe that minus seventy temperatures would be bad in daylight—not comparatively bad, when you see where you are going, where you are stepping, could read the compass without striking three or four boxes to find one dry match. In the mornings it took two men to get one man into his clothes, because sometimes our clothes were so frozen not even two men could bend them into the required shape."

"The journey," concluded Cherry-Garrard, "had beggared our language: no words could express its horror."

The reason the trio endured such hardship? Not gold. Not conquest. But merely to collect emperor penguin eggs for scientific study.

The annals of exploration prove that the journey was more important than the destination. Travel became a defining personal odyssey. The weak grew strong and the strong carried on. And for every Ross or Cherry-Garrard returning home to fanfare and acclaim, there were a dozen who perished or turned back, done in by the journey despite years of planning and physical preparation. Their loss was cause for despair, but nonetheless accepted as the price to be paid for unveiling the secret corridors of the globe. Left unsaid was that successful explorers seemed to possess physical and mental attributes that the unsuccessful lacked. These traits gave them an almost preternatural ability to withstand starvation, deprivation, torture, storms (both natural and personal), or just plain bad luck.

This was why, for instance, the RGS was loath to send a rescue party after Speke when he was "lost" in Africa, or to do the same when Sir John Franklin was overdue during his search for the Northwest Passage—this, even though the idiosyncratic navigator was one of the Society's founders. These explorers had gotten themselves into trouble, went the thinking; they would find a way to get themselves out. Speke survived this school of thought. Franklin did not.

The character attributes of successful explorers were the hardiest, most resilient set of traits any individual might hope to possess—among them curiosity, perseverance, and a sort of learned fearlessness. Those were traits anyone could use, in any walk of life or in any desperate situation. Yet they were never plumbed for commonalities, so that outsiders might similarly equip themselves.

This oversight became moot in 1979. Just a decade after Armstrong took his giant leap for mankind, the RGS awarded their gold medal to a Dr. David Stoddart for "contributions to geomorphology, the study of coral reefs, and the history of academic geography."

Stoddart was a Cambridge lecturer who had spent the summers studying the flora and fauna of the Aldabra Atoll in the Indian Ocean.* Stoddart's enthusiasm and perseverance were commendable. However, his gold medal marked a turning point in the history of the Royal Geographical Society. This was an award that had once been synonymous with travel into the unknown; with pushing mental, physical, and emotional limits. Now the RGS was awarding it to a research scientist. In doing so, those learned fellows were tacitly admitting that the age of exploration was done. Not just the age that began with King William's bequest; nor the age that

*Stoddart was also no dummy. The Aldabra Atoll is a tropical paradise in the Seychelles. It is virtually uninhabited and untouched by humans. Having a deserted tropical island to oneself sounds like a spectacular way to spend summer vacation.

began when "explorer" ceased to be a hunting term, and was first applied to those traveling to a new country in search of discoveries; nor even just the Victorian Age of Discovery, that most far-reaching of all epochs of exploration, with the heart-stopping adventures of Burton, Speke, and their search for the source of the Nile as its dramatic centerpiece.

No, this admission applied to all of exploration, beginning when the first human beings strode upright out of Africa and began propagating the Earth a hundred thousand or more years ago.

The Earth is a vast planet. It weighs some 6.6 sextillion tons. Measured around the equator, its circumference is 24,901.55 miles (polar circumference is 42 miles less). The average surface temperature is a mild 59 degrees Fahrenheit, but the Libyan Desert can hit 140 and the South Pole can sink to that same temperature on the minus side. More germane to the topic of exploration, the Earth's surface area is 196,800,000 square miles, of which 57,300,000 is dry land.

Now the RGS was saying every last inch had been explored. There was nothing left to find. Just to prove that Stoddart's win wasn't an aberration, the RGS proceeded to award the next twenty-five consecutive gold medals to men of science. Nowadays, instead of "for his perseverance and success in exploring the territory and investigating the resources of British Guyana," as Robert H. Schomburg's citation read in 1840, the wording is more along the lines of, "for contributions to the development of process-based geomorphology," as when Professor Mike Kirby won in 1999, or Professor Brian Robson's "contributions to urban geography" in 2000.

Interestingly, a Dr. David Livingstone won in 2011, "for the encouragement and promotion of historical geography," a pursuit no doubt unaccompanied by the dysentery, parasites, and lion attack that the previous winner of the same name endured in Africa while earning his gold medal in 1855.

The passing of exploration went unnoted. There was no deep collective breath to frame the world's most adventurous time span with proper perspective. It was a glaring oversight. No other group of achievers has been so bold—or foolhardy. Explorers mapped the Sahara's burning sands, charted the mountains of Tibet, and rediscovered lost civilizations. They died of frostbite, expelled their innards through amoebic dysentery, and sometimes simply disappeared. They did those things and so much more, making the world, through their travails and hardships, a better place. "This discipline of suffering—of great suffering," as philosopher Friedrich Nietzche once wrote, "know ye not that it is only this discipline that has produced the elevation of all humanity?"

They were dreamers, botanists, entrepreneurs, librarians, dropouts, missionaries, captains, widows, and more. Their stations in life were diverse and often unremarkable. A few were wealthy, though most were not. Some were comfortable with solitude, while others traveled in groups. An intriguing percentage were second children. Some were gay. Many undertook just one great journey in their life, a two- or six-year season of extreme personal risk before returning home to comfortable obscurity. Others made exploration their life's work. Few thought themselves particularly brave. "It requires far less courage to be an explorer than to be a chartered accountant," wrote mountain climber Peter Fleming. "The courage which enables you to face the prospect of sitting on a high stool in a smoky town adding up figures over a period of years is definitely higher, as well as a more useful sort of courage, than any which the explorer may be called upon to display."

Consider this description of polar explorer Robert Falcon Scott. "Scott was the strongest combination of a strong man in a strong body that I have ever known," wrote Apsley Cherry-Garrard, who accompanied Scott on his doomed voyage. "And this because he was so weak! Naturally so peevish, highly-strung, irritable, depressed and moody. Practically such a conquest of himself, such vitality, such push and determination, and withal in himself such personal and magnetic charm. His triumphs are many—but the Pole was not by any means the greatest of them. Surely the greatest of them was that he conquered his weaker self and became the strong leader whom we went to follow and whom we came to love."

Scott, like other explorers, set out to challenge himself, and in the process changed the world. Their personal struggles comprise the history of exploration, a powerful study of human nature highlighting the potential within all of us to do something far beyond that which we think ourselves capable. That's why looking back at these individuals and their achievements is so worthwhile. The RGS was somewhat right—bar perhaps the bottom of several deep-sea trenches, and some epic caves, the Earth has physically been explored. But that doesn't mean the Earth is devoid of challenge. In our lives, we all move forward into the unknown, making each of us just one of the seven billion explorers on the planet. And the men and women I want to write about in this book are not only pathmakers who helped redraw the maps; their lives are maps themselves.

In this way, there is a universal connection between explorers and just about anyone who has ever stepped outside their comfort zone to challenge themselves. What are we capable of accomplishing? What are our limits? How far is too far? How far is not far enough?

This quest for potential spans the centuries. It is the link between Christopher Columbus and Steve Jobs. It is the root source of failure, for to fail at something one must first make an attempt. Potential, however, is also the root source of smashing, breathtaking, world-changing success. Wilfrid Noyce, a British mountain climber who was part of the first successful ascent of Mount Everest, once wrote, "Why do we do it? I think the reasons are many, and that one of them is simply that it is part of the human nature to want to 'prove' yourself, to show yourself that you could do something you thought impossible."

So the history of exploration is not just an interconnected series of journeys, but also a powerful study of the human condition. There is an explorer within each of us, silently longing to climb our own personal Everest.

The commonality can most easily be seen in the seven common traits that all explorers possessed: curiosity, hope, passion, courage, independence, self-discipline, and perseverance. Explorers didn't just own those traits; they also displayed them in specific order over the course of a journey. Take away one—just one—and an expedition was doomed to failure.

These seven traits are also vital to all of us, in the challenges we face each day, as tools to help us through our own wilderness wanderings. Motivational theorists argue that all successful human endeavors follow the same path from curiosity through to perseverance that the explorers did—and in the same order. Not only that, but navigating this path is developmentally vital to ensuring feelings of personal fulfillment and wellness. "This construct describes the natural inclination toward exploration," wrote Dr. Richard Ryan in *American Psychologist*, describing the Theory of Intrinsic Motivation, which explores the roots of curiosity. "It is essential to cognitive and social development and represents a principal source of enjoyment and vitality through life."

Psychologists at the University of Pennsylvania went a step further, stating that these attributes "improve quality of life and prevent the pathologies that arise when life is barren and meaningless," and are "the positive features that make life worth living."*

The seven traits of an explorer are more than just random traits shared by hardy souls. They are the building blocks of well-being and success, applicable to each and every one of us, every day of our lives. In them, we glimpse the potential for greatness residing inside us all.

But it should also be noted there is a reason that explorers needed to find that greatness far from the social restrictions and expectations of society. This makes them very difficult people to study, and even more difficult to see past their limitations. Explorers were famous for burning down their own lives—and the lives of others. They were outcasts. They were terrible with money. They loved the wrong people.

They *were* the wrong people.†

And yet, they somehow achieved feats beyond belief or measure. We all have limitations, and we all have moments of messy behavior. So don't examine the lives of explorers for morality lessons, half measures, or social cues. Instead, see explorers as men and women bent on finding their own per-

*Researchers Martin Seligman and Mihaly Csikszentmihalyi, leading voices in the study of positive psychology, framed the traits as hope, wisdom, creativity, future-mindedness, courage, spirituality, responsibility, and perseverance.
†Paraphrased from a speech given by Bruce Springsteen while accepting an award on February 19, 2013. He was speaking about musicians. Given that explorers have frequently been labeled as the rock stars of their time, the comparison is apt.

sonal greatness by fulfilling their potential, and study the steps they took to get there, succeeding in spite of their limitations. What better place to look for guidance as we divine the path through our own tangled lives than the men and women who have already blazed that trail?

"Exploration," as Apollo astronaut Frank Borman once noted, "is really the essence of the human spirit."

Which brings us back to Speke.

CURIOSITY

1

The air reeked of squalor and coal dust as twenty-seven-year-old Jack Speke stepped off the P&O* steamer from Calcutta in search of his first African adventure. Flies were everywhere. It was mid-September 1854, and the miserable port of Aden, with its barren volcanic landscape, unremitting heat, and towering piles of coal, was to be a brief stopover. The refueling hub at the southern tip of the Arabian Peninsula was

*The Peninsular and Oriental Steam Navigation Company was founded in 1822, and reigned as Britain's leading shipping firm until after World War II. It still exists, having been sold in 2006 for £3.9 billion to the container giant Dubai Ports World.

just 300 miles across the Red Sea from the mysterious and uncharted land so often referred to as "the Dark Continent." All Speke had to do was find a ship that would transport him to the other side. His goal was hunting big game, and he had no qualms about traveling alone. In fact, he reveled in the solitude.

Speke was born on May 4, 1827, in rural England, into a lineage that suggested anything but a life of adventure. Jack Speke was a loner who performed poorly in school, and stumbled with the social graces. Little about him suggested he would become an explorer, let alone one of such surpassing greatness that a nation whose vast global empire was built upon the discovery and conquest of previously uncharted spots on the map would erect a towering monument in his name.

In a word, Jack Speke possessed that most vital requirement for becoming an explorer: he was ordinary.

By his early twenties, Speke was just a shade under six feet tall, brown-haired, long-limbed, and prone to anxiety—unless he was hunting, whereupon Speke became the picture of steely resolve. His family had owned an estate in the British countryside since Norman times, giving him a societal edge that he used to great effect throughout his life. His mother was domineering and his father had no interest in leaving his manor to run for political office, like so many influential men of his time. But Jack Speke had no such qualms. He left home at seventeen because it was clear that his older brother was the apple of his father William's eye. Remaining at Jordans, the family home in Somerset, would have been a daily reminder that none of the green pastures and hills on which he so loved to hunt would ever be passed on to him.

So, with the intercession of the Duke of Wellington, Speke was commissioned and packed off to India. There he fought in the First Anglo-Sikh War, was heavily decorated for courage under fire, earned a reputation for keeping to himself, abstaining from drink most of the time, keeping his hands off the local women, and taking solitary hunting adventures into the wilds of India and Tibet.

Though his penchant for solitude and heady independence made Speke a poor choice for a military man, the Royal Army was the making of him.

By 1854, after ten long years of service, Speke had accrued a massive three years of leave. Having also used that time to save as much of his salary as possible, Speke possessed the time and the means to wander across the plains of Africa, hunting game and collecting plant and bird specimens for his private collection.

If the otherwise virtuous Speke had a fault, it was the zeal in which he pursued those shooting forays. He shot in the manner of the great buffalo hunters of the American West, killing any new and unique animal that wandered into his path. His native bearers then toted the heads and skins back to his outpost, whereupon they were shipped home to Jordans for display in the small family museum. The carcasses were often left where they fell. This might have been considered enterprising on the Great Plains, where some sixty million bison were wiped out in less than forty years,* but among his fellow British officers, Speke's obsession with these solitary hunts marked him as an outsider. On September 4, just one day after finishing his ten years of service in India and attaining the rank of captain, Speke boarded the P&O bound for Aden. After exhaustively overhunting the Asian subcontinent, he had every intention of doing the same in Africa. Before leaving India he had purchased "cheap guns, revolving pistols, swords, cheap cutlery of all sorts, beads, cotton stuffs of a variety of kinds, and sewing material, to the amount of £390 sterling" for the purpose of bartering with Africans along the way.

For a man who had taken fire from the militant Sikhs in pitched military battles at Rámnagar, Sadullápur, Chilianwala, and Gujarat, Speke seems to have been possessed of a powerful naïveté. One did not merely wander alone into Africa and amble about the countryside, no matter how well armed. At Somaliland, for instance, the point of landfall closest to Aden, there lived a tribe colloquially known as "the penis-cutting people," for their fondness of emasculating their victims. European missionaries who had made the mistake of venturing

---

*Some hunters took as many as 250 buffalo a day. The new transcontinental railroad took advantage of the great herds by letting passengers fire their weapons from trains. The fallen animals were left to rot, which infuriated the Native American tribes who depended upon them as a food source, and became a primary reason for waging war on incoming settlers.

solo into Africa were routinely killed, or sometimes held captive by a tribal king for the rest of their lives. The British aura of supremacy, which had protected Speke during his hunting forays into the relatively peaceful tribal regions of the Punjab and Himalayas, was nowhere to be seen in Africa. Other than Cape Town, some four thousand miles south of Somaliland, the British presence in sub-Saharan Africa was limited to an exploration party currently making its way along the Zambezi River and led by David Livingstone—a dyspeptic former missionary and physician who was hardly the embodiment of military might.

We'll get to Livingstone later, for he plays a crucial role in the drama of Speke and Burton. But for now the fact remains that Speke did not possess a clear command of the facts when it came to Africa. Call it the entitlement of a man raised in wealth, or the mind-set of a man just returned from a decade of subjugating a nation to the will of Britain and Queen Victoria, but Speke was deeply out of touch with reality.

2

Thankfully, the British political agent in Aden, Colonel James Outram, told him so. Informing Speke that the Somali were "of such a wild and inhospitable nature that no stranger could possibly live among them," Outram specifically forbade Speke from attempting the journey. And without Outram's blessing, Speke's quest was as good as over.

This saga might have ended there, were it not for the presence of another would-be traveler enduring the heat and flies of Aden. Richard Francis Burton had been there since May, his heart set on exploring the interior of Somaliland. At the time of Speke's arrival, the intense and often contentious Burton was embroiled in a bitter feud with Outram over the political agent's refusal to let him venture into Africa.

Burton was a proven adventurer, already famous (and increasingly infamous) throughout England. He had placed his life at great risk by disguising himself as a Muslim pilgrim and successfully traveling to the holy city of Mecca just a year earlier. The punishment for a non-Muslim caught attempting such a deception is death, and Burton was forced to don several disguises, affect several different dialects, and even undergo circumcision to make sure he could pass for a Muslim. Once, while urinating standing up instead of squatting in the Arab custom, he almost gave himself away. But Burton talked his way out of that awkward moment, completed his pilgrimage, and became instantly revered throughout England for his audacious courage.

On the infamous side, Burton, who had enlisted in the army after being kicked out of Oxford's Trinity College in 1842, had been charged with investigating the brothels of Karachi during his army service in India. The resulting report effectively ended all chance of a serious military career, as it incriminated several high-ranking British officers on charges of having sex with young men and small children. And while

Burton was a proficient fencer, falconer, and linguist,* the charge that would follow him the rest of his life was that of hedonist—for while Burton was investigating the brothels, there was also ample evidence that he mightily enjoyed them. Burton certainly didn't help matters later in life by translating the Kama Sutra into English and starting a secret society to publish and circulate erotic literature at a time when the Obscene Publications Act of 1857 meant prison time for violators.

All that being said, Burton's Somaliland Expedition was down a man, due to the sudden death of his old friend, Dr. J. Ellerton Stocks, while back home in London. The cause of death was apoplexy, which at the time meant any sort of unexplained instant demise ranging from heart attack to cerebral aneurysm. A far worse fate might have awaited Stocks in Africa, as Burton and Speke would soon learn for themselves. But the bottom line was that Burton was in a spot of bother. He needed a new hand for his expedition, and was glad to overlook the obvious societal and personal gaps between the two of them. Once it was agreed that Speke might join the expedition, the two men set to work on changing Outram's mind.

On the surface, Jack Speke and Dick Burton had little

---

*Burton spoke fluent Arabic, Gujurati, Hindustani, Punjabi, Sindhi, Marathi, and Persian. However, owing to his outcast status within the Royal Army, he was failed when he took the exam that would qualify him as an Arab translator.

in common. But there was the one trait they shared in abundance, and this made them fast friends. The trait was evidenced not just by their determination to explore an uncharted land, and their vast range of personal hobbies, but also their unrepentant desire to seek the unknown at all cost.

It is known as curiosity.

3

Human curiosity is a private thing, the satisfying of a need. It was curiosity that motivated explorers to venture forth. "A desire," as Venetian Ludovico di Varthema noted in the sixteenth century, "to behold the kingdoms of the world."

Curiosity beats within all of us, for mankind is innately inquisitive. In childhood our curiosities are vast, leading us to wonder, often aloud, about the world and the heavens. For most of us those curiosities narrow to the practical as we grow older, until questions about the vast unknown beyond our daily routine occupy a neglected corner of the brain, trotted out only while reading travel brochures or gazing at constellations.

Explorers were different. Their curiosity had a boundlessness that never diminished. It inhabited their psyches and their dreams, allowing them to approach each day with a sense of wonder. And in that wonder, they attained the epic. "Then, too, there was the fascination of seeing the very heart of the Himalayas," wrote Francis Younghusband in 1887, during his epic walk from Peking to Bombay, "as we should have crossed their entire breadth on the way to India. And all combined was one grand project—this idea of striking boldly out from Peking to penetrate to India—that of itself inspired enthusiasm and roused every spark of exploring ardor in me."

Curiosity drew explorers into the magnetic pull of new places, people, objects, rituals, and vistas. They longed to learn more, and often became so immersed that these lands became a sort of second home. With this familiarity, the explorer was compelled to push on, to begin the cycle of leaving normal and striking into the unknown all over again. "Already I dropped back into the desert as if it were my own place," Gertrude Bell wrote while wandering across central Arabia before World War I. "Silence and solitude fell around you like an impenetrable veil."

Curiosity is a sign of high intelligence, high self-esteem, and autonomy. There is a great connection between curiosity and creativity. And while curiosity peaks in childhood, when the entire world is new, a lifelong habit of curiosity is empowering. Studies have shown that elderly adults who are high in curiosity have longer lives, perhaps because the autonomy that accompanies curiosity develops its own skill set of survival. On the other hand, individuals who whether by nature or nurture shut off the natural human instinct to explore the world in a physical and intellectual manner, often succumb to lethargy.

Curiosity plays such a powerful role in all great accomplishments that there is evidence the act of discovery triggers the human body's narcotic-like dopamine chemical to flood the brain, a positive stimulus that ensures an individual would want to re-create the sensation through newer and greater discoveries. It's worth noting that abnormal dopamine levels also play a role in drug addiction, schizophrenia, and Attention Deficit Hyperactivity Disorder (ADHD)—all of which seem to appear more among explorers and creative geniuses than among the vast majority of the population.

But the body also splits curiosity into the two camps of "wanting" and "liking."

This is vital.

When one merely wants something, but does not like the sensation, there can be "no motivation for further reward."*

Though they were only just beginning to learn about its rewards, Burton and Speke knew a great deal about curiosity—the desire to know as much as humanly possible about the known world was almost like a parlor game in London, best denoted in the number of special academic societies devoted to every field of study from numismatics to horticulture and geology. There would even be a society devoted to aeronautics in 1866, almost a half century before man learned to fly. The best of these collectives would receive the blessing of Queen Victoria, and earned the right to append the sobriquet "Royal Society" to their name. None of these, of course, would ever transcend the magnificence of the original royal

*Kent C. Berridge, *Physiology & Behavior*, 16 February 2009.

society, that of the Royal Society of London for the Improve-
ment of Natural Knowledge—or just the Royal Society, as it
is known to this day. The legacy of their relentless pursuit of
knowledge is evidenced in the modern age, and the NASA
Mars rover named *Curiosity*, tasked with slowly surveying
the Red Planet in much the same way as the Royal Society,
founded in 1660, and its nascent, exploration-centric offspring
the Royal Geographical Society once surveyed Earth.

So Speke and Burton were quite aware of the concept of
curiosity. But they knew absolutely nothing about dopamine,
which would not be discovered until 1957. All Speke and Burton knew was that every now and again they were overcome
by an unexplained euphoria when they did something special.

But as little as they knew about dopamine or the chemis-
try of their brains, Jack Speke and Dick Burton knew even less
about the interior of Africa.

It was this lack of knowledge that fired their curiosity with
such a deep and immeasurable force that they were willing to
risk their very lives just to unlock Africa's secrets.

But for curiosity, the amazing story of Burton and Speke
would have never come to pass.

They might never have had the chance to venture into Africa, however, were it not for a single grisly murder that took
place before either man was born. The executed man's name
was James Cook. He had no middle initial. And he died far
from Africa, almost halfway around the world, in an ironically
idyllic clear blue Pacific cove.

4

On the western edge of the Pacific Rim, quietly nestled between a golf course and a former US Navy bombing range in Southern California, there stands a small and rather overlooked monument to curiosity. It comes in the form of a plaque noting that on July 25, 1769, Spanish explorer Gaspar de Portola led a party of soldiers inland from where their ship was anchored in the Pacific Ocean, searching for new sites to build Catholic missions on the California coast. Leaving the beach in the early morning, they marched in ragged formation up a low valley. Oaks and sycamores provided shade from the searing summer sun. They stepped carefully, wary of rattlesnakes, mountain lions, and grizzly bears. A small dry creekbed paralleled their path, but water was nowhere to be found.

After three hours Portola called a halt. His men stretched out in the shade and took off the steel morion helmets that made sweat roll down their faces in great salty rivulets. One of them lost his gun, a small blunderbuss known as a trabuco. It would never be found—at least not by Portola or that unfortunate soldier—and to this day, that resting spot is known as the Plano Trabuco.

At precisely the same moment Portola's men were taking a rest from the dry heat, a thirty-five-year-old former Quaker named Daniel Boone was 2,500 miles to the east in Tennessee, traveling through the Appalachian Mountains. He was soon building a road through the Cumberland Gap that would become known as the Wilderness Road, bringing about the westward expansion that led to the purchase of the Louisiana Territory and to the opening of the American frontier.

On the same date, in what is now the African nation of Sudan, Scotsman James Bruce was on the verge of laying eyes on the source of a tributary known as the Blue Nile, but still years from tumbling down a flight of stairs to his death while answering the door in his own home.

Finally, a fourth explorer was changing the world at the exact same time. Lieutenant James Cook was sailing away from Tahiti on his first circumnavigation of the globe aboard His Majesty's Bark (HMB) *Endeavour*, just months away from charting the coast of New Zealand and then inadvertently discovering the east coast of Australia.

Portola, meanwhile, enjoyed his resting spot so much that he ordered his men to make camp there for the night. Come morning, having found water, he chose to build a small fort of mud and grass. It would become the first Spanish fort built in what is now Orange County, California. During World War II, the US Navy used the grasslands of the Plano Trabuco as a bombing range, but the remains of Portola's simple fort can still be seen. A golf course and a housing development now stand just two hundred yards away, and a simple gravel trail winds past the monument marking the spot. The fort is just half of one wall now, protected from the elements by a corrugated tin shack. But it is still there, and that counts for something rather marvelous. The plaque that has been erected on the site informs passing hikers that this mundane location is a link to a chain of events that changed mankind's view of the planet on which we live.

Not in his wildest dreams could Portola have foreseen that his explorations would one day culminate in suburbia. Nor could Cook have envisioned glass and steel cities like Sydney or Auckland on lands he discovered; nor Boone the interstate highway running through the Cumberland Gap (or the coonskin cap fad, or a Disney TV show); nor could Bruce envision the amazing fact that the Blue Nile is still very much the same ripping, lonesome waterway he traced more than two hundred years ago. They were ordinary men doing extraordinary things, putting one foot in front of another in the name of exploration. They lived in the moment. Even if they had known what those same lands would look like two and a quarter centuries later, they wouldn't have spent much time thinking about it. Any distraction from the moment-by-moment process of exploration could have meant a mistake that might lead to death.

Of those four explorers who were simultaneously charting the planet on July 25, 1769, Cook would prove the most pivotal. He mapped almost the entire Pacific Rim, including what is now Oregon, Washington, British Columbia, and Alaska. He discovered the continent of Antarctica. He sailed the Pacific in a random pattern until he stumbled upon the Hawaiian Islands, among many others. The stoic Cook endured everything from 100-foot waves to shipwreck as he sailed around the world twice. Most important of all, he was so taken with his calling that he spent almost the entire last decade of his life at sea. It was a heady time for a man born the second son of an itinerant farm laborer, and it is proper and fitting that Cook be remembered for the courage, fastidiousness, and enduring curiosity that led him to amble slowly around the Pacific on his three epic voyages, discovering as many new lands as possible before inevitably sailing back to the London dockyards to report on all he had seen and done.

And yet Cook's greatest legacy is his murder. For it was his savage execution that unwittingly began the great Victorian age of discovery taking place between 1779 and 1922.

5

It all went wrong in an otherwise idyllic anchorage off the coast of Hawaii known as Kealakekua Bay, a spot now favored by snorkelers and tour boats. There, the fifty-year-old Cook was set upon by a mob of locals and stabbed more than one hundred times. As his crew watched helplessly from the decks of his flagship, *Resolution*, their captain's body was then borne off into the jungle by Hawaiian warriors. There, the local chieftains cut his newly dead heart from his chest and ate it raw. The rest of the body was lowered into a pit and slow-cooked like a pig. Cook's bones were later pulled from the coals and scattered about the island. When the crew of *Resolution* demanded that Cook's remains be returned, the only items worthy of burial were a left hand and a shoe. To this day, his bones have not been found.

Until Cook's death on February 14, 1779—Valentine's Day, ironically, given what became of his heart—the focus of Britain's global exploration was the ocean. By charting the seas, and finding new lands to colonize and exploit, that small island nation slowly began assembling what would one day be known as the British Empire—spanning the globe so completely that the sun never set on it.

By the time Cook was murdered in 1779, it was felt that he had found all there was to find on the high seas. Based on this belief, Britain officially ceased all voyages of exploration in 1781.

This didn't deter adventurers, scientists, and other thinkers in the least. Their focus turned to privately funded land-based journeys. The typical British explorer was no longer a military man, but a private voyager. Instead of ships, these explorers journeyed on foot, or the back of an ass or a camel, threading their narrow paths into the spots on the maps shaded dark and labeled "Unknown." Some sought gold or silver. A few had designs on colonization. But for the most part these men and women just wanted to go someplace no one else had ever been, or to help others get there so they might also know about it.

The one place that held the public in thrall like no other was Africa—unknown, unexplored, infinitely dangerous Africa.

So it came to pass on Monday, June 9, 1788, that nine wealthy, hard-drinking Englishmen known as the Saturday's Club met in a rented upstairs room at the St. Alban's Pub, on a dingy cobbled alley of a street just a block south of Piccadilly.

It might have just as easily been called the Curiosity Club, because the men who filled that small room were insatiable in their desire to know all there was about the world around them. Their sole intention was to discuss their greatest thirst of all—that for knowledge. Sir William Fordyce was a physician who had published books on venereal disease. Thirty-three-year-old Irishman Francis Rawdon had just returned from fighting in the American War of Independence and would soon be named governor-general of India. Seventy-year-old general Rufus Conway was retired from the military and had taken up the study of botany and linguistics to pass the time. The Earl of Galloway was fond of spouting the latest theories on subjects as diverse as slavery and agriculture. Henry Beaufoy was a Member of Parliament. Andrew Stuart used to be. Sir Adam Ferguson was His Majesty's commissioner of trade and plantations. And William Pulteney was merely rich.

Their soft-spoken leader, and the most curious thinker of them all, was Sir Joseph Banks. Playboy, bon vivant, philanthropist, naturalist, erstwhile world traveler, and incumbent president of Europe's most esteemed intellectual body, the Royal Society, Banks had lived forty-five intense years, collecting critics and worshipers the world over. He sailed with Cook on the famed *Endeavour* circumnavigation, acquiring plants and sexual consorts on the newly discovered islands of the South Pacific; funded the ill-fated *Bounty* voyage after befriending a former ship's master named William Bligh; and convinced the British government that the new continent of Australia was the ideal location to send Britain's prison population, replacing the legendary hellholes of Georgia and Florida that had been lost to the newly anointed "Americans." Indeed, as the naturalist took his seat at St. Alban's, Sir Arthur Philip's First Fleet and its inaugural load of prisoners were constructing the new penal colony. Philip would name it for Thomas Townshend, a nobleman friend of Banks's who also went by the name Viscount Sydney.

Philip should have named it for Banks.

One day he would be portly, but in June 1788 Joseph Banks was merely robust. His reddish-brown hair had almost all gone gray. There was still plenty of it, however, and the naturalist wore it in a ponytail tied with a ribbon. He was shy at formal dinner parties, but had a reputation for leaning in when the discussion caught his fancy, fixing his piercing blue eyes on the person with whom he was speaking. He dressed in a subdued fashion, although the insightful would notice that the ruffled cuffs of Banks's shirts were made by the finest tailors on Bond Street. This was made possible by the considerable fortune Banks had inherited in his teens, back in the days before he discovered that his hunger for knowledge was even greater than his formidable hunger for sex. Very often the agenda for a meeting of the Saturday's Club combined a little of both: dinner, scholarly debate, and then the arrival of the finest local prostitutes, whereupon the doors were locked from the inside for the duration.

But not on the second Monday in June 1788. On this night, Banks's preoccupation with knowledge won out. Wine was served, then a hot meal. Once the dinner plates had been removed, Banks hoisted his wineglass and proposed a toast to, of all places, Africa.

6

Specifically, Banks wanted to know more about it.

The shape of the continent was that of an eastward-facing skull, as had been known by mapmakers for centuries. In fact, the entire coastline had been charted, and the southern tip had even become a trade enclave known as Cape Town. But the remainder of Africa, an area so vast that all of Europe could fit inside it three times, was a massive question mark. Little was known about rivers like the Niger and Nile, except that they flowed thousands of miles from the interior of Africa before emptying into the seas. No one knew from where they came. There was talk that they were the same river. There were theories of fabled lands like the biblical desert kingdom of Meroe; and Timbuktu, a so-called city of gold. No one knew for sure.

A smattering of expeditions had been launched into Africa over the centuries, but their results weren't completely believed: the secretive Portuguese claimed that a pair of their explorers had walked across central Africa from east to west in the sixteenth century; and a Scot named James Bruce was currently boasting that he had found a source of the Nile. Banks, along with other great thinkers such as Edmund Burke, Horace Walpole, and the aging Dr. Samuel Johnson, didn't believe him. Bruce's claims were even mocked in a new book about a fallacious adventurer named Baron Munchhausen.

Nothing of substance, in the minds of the Saturday's Club, was known about the interior of sub-Saharan Africa. Banks proposed they remedy that immediately. His plan was that they spin off to form a new society.

All agreed. A resolution was written to give the new undertaking suitable gravitas. "As the vast continent of Africa, notwithstanding the efforts of the ancients, and the wishes of the moderns, is still in a measure unexplored, the members of this Club do form themselves into an association for promoting the discovery of the inland parts of that quarter of the world."

The African Association, as the nine called this new undertaking (abbreviated from the mouthier "Association for Promoting the Discovery of the Interior Parts of Africa"), would not be a mere social gathering. They would pinpoint areas of Africa they wished to see explored, find the man capable of making the journey, then fund and equip the entire expedition.

"Of the objects of inquiry which engage our attention the most, there are none, perhaps, that so much excite continued curiosity. From childhood to age; none that the learned or unlearned so equally wish to investigate," Henry Beaufoy, the Member of Parliament, wrote of Africa.

Curiosity was something of an epidemic in London society at the time, thanks to the Age of Reason. Once merely a philosophical movement dedicated to rationalism, equality, and political freedom, it had expanded to become a search for all forms of scholarly wisdom. Possession of knowledge was so trendy as to be an aphrodisiac, in the manner of wealth or power. There were societies and associations for every conceivable form of curiosity, from the Linnaean Association and their study of botany, to a group dedicated to investigating the high cost of butchers' meat. But the African Association's aim was to be different. It would be curiosity in action rather than a passive sifting and reappraisal of current knowledge; a thoughtful step from the wish for an answer to its zealous pursuit.

To Banks, curiosity also carried an incumbent nostalgia. Once upon a time he would have proposed himself as the man to represent the Association in Africa. But gone were the days when he set forth into the wilds. The onset of gout and a fondness for fancy breakfasts in his Soho Square mansion made that unrealistic. But Banks could well recall the thrill of hands-on discovery, just as he could also vividly remember his fear on the day he first went to sea with Cook in 1768. Banks had been rowed, hung over, to where *Endeavour* lay at anchor off Plymouth. He had then demanded the ship's great cabin as his living quarters, an outrageous request to which Cook, a lifelong commoner, quietly acquiesced in the name of class consciousness.

Banks had been a newcomer to science at the time. He considered this lower-class sailor, who had only recently been elevated to a commissioned rank, to be nothing more than the dim-witted driver of the ship that would lead him to glory. But over the course of their two years together, Cook quietly asserted his authority—and his brilliance. In the process he indoctrinated Banks into the joys of exploration. The tall, introspective lieutenant (Cook would not be named a captain until after their return) did not travel in linear fashion, sprinting around the globe. He wandered the seas, tirelessly searching for the unknown just over the horizon. When a new land was discovered, that simple wandering was supplanted by an even deeper level of curiosity. Coastlines were sounded and charted until every last inch was recorded. Local peoples were observed. Plants were pressed. Animal specimens were preserved. As the French admiral Jean François de la Perouse so famously noted of Cook, "He carried out work that was so all-encompassing that there was little for his successors to do but admire it."*

By observing Cook, Banks had learned the importance

---

*Ironically, La Perouse was lost at sea at almost the exact same time the African Association was being formed. On January 26, 1788, he arrived at Botany Bay, where Cook had made landfall in Australia. But Sir Arthur Philip and the British First Fleet had arrived two days earlier, thus of indulging curiosity. Then, as now, it was the only vehicle for pushing exploration to its absolute limit. He would later adopt this practice as his own, assuring his lasting fame as a naturalist, while also learning that the more he knew, the less he knew. Curiosity and knowledge are like fire and fuel: more knowledge does not satisfy curiosity, but stokes the flames, leading to an even greater need to know what lies over the horizon.

7

If the African Association was going to take the lead in exploring the continent's interior, then Banks expected the job to be carried out with Cook-like thoroughness. The key to achieving this goal was to find a man with the late captain's relentless desire to know the unknown.

Word about the African Association made its way around London overnight. Within a week they were inundated by applications to lead the inaugural expedition. Banks ignored them all. He'd already chosen his man. Most preposterously, given how poorly the English fared in the recent War of Rebellion (as the Revolutionary War was known in Britain), Banks chose an American.

John Ledyard possessed an abundance of refined curiosity—

---

denying France the new continent. La Perouse sailed from Botany Bay on March 10. His ships sank in a storm two months later.

or at least seemed to. He was the son of a sea captain, and he liked it very much when people referred to him as "the first American explorer."

Ledyard's life, like that of Banks, was an amazement. And as with Banks, the defining moment of Ledyard's life up to 1788 had been while at sea with Captain Cook. In his early twenties he had dropped out of Dartmouth College in New Hampshire and impulsively sailed to Gibraltar to enlist in the Royal Marines, with the goal of traveling around the world. In 1778, at age twenty-seven, Ledyard had been posted as a corporal on the legendary *Resolution* for Cook's third and final voyage of exploration. Ledyard was a literate fellow, an unusual sort of behavior for a royal marine at the time. He kept a journal of his years at sea with Cook. The Admiralty confiscated his writings for national security reasons upon his return to London. But Ledyard rewrote his journal from memory after leaving the Royal Marines, particularly the events surrounding Cook's murder. The resulting book, *A Journal of Captain Cook's Last Voyage*, became a best seller. Ledyard, like Burton and Speke eighty years later, soon became a famous explorer.

The problem—the unscratched itch—was that Ledyard had not yet completed his voyage around the world. So he spent his royalties on a trip to Paris, where he hoped to raise funding for a ship to captain and a crew to lead. Ledyard was unsuccessful. He persisted. There was nothing particularly special about him beyond a barrel chest and a resolute desire to brave the unknown. He was smallish and unimaginative, prone to delusions of grandeur, lacking in discretion, and bound to do or say anything to draw attention to himself. When he chanced to meet an American admirer named Thomas Jefferson, who proposed a radically different sort of journey, Ledyard was all ears.

The future president of the United States was something of an exploration aficionado. Not only did Jefferson possess a collection of world maps dating back to 1507, but among his holdings were copies of Cook's personal journals. Jefferson, who was in Paris for a five-year diplomatic posting when he and Ledyard first met, was especially curious about the lands between North America's Pacific and Atlantic coasts. Jefferson suggested to Ledyard a journey very similar to what he would propose to Meriwether Lewis and William Clark fifteen years later: a walk from one side of the Americas to the other. Ledyard was intrigued, but still thinking in terms of circumnavigation. He countered Jefferson's plan with one of his own: a walk around the world. More a combination of walking and sailing, what Ledyard proposed was a journey that would begin in London, take him across Russia, have him sail the Bering Strait, then walk clear across North America to Washington, DC, before sailing on to London again. All he needed, Ledyard wrote to Jefferson, was the permission of Russia's empress, Catherine the Great. If she allowed him to cross her vast nation unmolested, the journey could begin.

Jefferson gingerly approached Russian officials in Paris to make a formal request. He was rebuffed. Catherine was suspicious that America had designs on the Siberian fur trade (true in Ledyard's case). Describing Ledyard's plan as "chimerical," she refused her blessing.

Ledyard went anyway.

In the autumn of 1786 he set off on foot from London. He carried a small pack, little money, slept on floors and in pastures, and begged food. By January of the following year he had reached Stockholm. The Baltic Sea, that narrow inlet separating Scandinavia from northern Europe, typically freezes solid in the winter, when temperatures reach far below zero. Ledyard's plan was to march across the ice, then follow the Gulf of Finland to St. Petersburg. All told, it would be a distance of 400 miles.

But the weather was unusually warm that year. The Baltic didn't freeze. Ledyard pressed on anyway, enduring a march north through Sweden, up above the Arctic Circle into Lapland, then down through Norway before finally crossing into Russia and reaching St. Petersburg at the onset of spring. He had traveled 1,200 miles in less than two months, an amazing pace for a journey in the dead of winter.

Ledyard knew that he needed to maintain that speed to avoid spending the following winter in Siberia—an unexplored region where the temperatures were only slightly milder, and the thick forests were filled with bears and tigers. Alone, nearly penniless, living off the land, Ledyard pressed forward with his solitary march. By September 18, 1787, Ledyard was so far across Siberia and close to the Sea of Okhotsk that he found himself contemplating a future return to the area to make his fortune in the fur trade.

Then the vast legacy of Captain Cook entered his life once again. Ledyard met up with Joseph Billings, a former able seaman on *Resolution* who now worked as a trader for the Russians. Billings pretended to befriend his old acquaintance, but then had him arrested under orders from a righteously enraged Catherine the Great. After walking more than 6,800 miles through some of the world's most harsh terrain, Ledyard was turned around. Russian officials accused him of spying and marched him all the way back to the Polish border. Upon cutting his ropes to set him free, the Russians promised to hang Ledyard the instant he showed his face in Russia again.

The smart thing for Ledyard to do would have been to scamper to his great admirer Jefferson and explain his side of the story. But Ledyard skipped Paris. Instead, he severed his relationship with Jefferson by turning to America's former enemy for assistance, thinking Britain alone had the power to make his exploration dreams a reality. Ledyard made a beeline from the Polish border to London. And not just to any place in London, but to the epicenter of British exploration: Joseph Banks's town house. Ledyard arrived in May 1788, ragged and destitute, begging relief even as he trumpeted his achievements. Three weeks later Banks presented Ledyard's credentials to the African Association, proposing him as their new expedition leader. Despite Ledyard's shortcomings, the American's relationship to Cook and the epic nature of his undertakings won the day. Ledyard chose to see Africa as a continuation of his around-the-world trek rather than a deviation.

There is a great possibility Ledyard would have been the first man to discover the sources of the Nile and Niger, as the Association hoped. He certainly had that dogged ability to put one foot in front of the other, morning after morning, no matter how awful the conditions. The world would still have his name on the tips of their tongues, if that were the case. If only in America, "Ledyard" might have a more epic ring than "Lewis and Clark."

But Ledyard never made it past Cairo. Somewhere during his journeys Ledyard changed. His deep curiosity was replaced by a sense of self-righteousness—characteristics that would one day define Burton. The pauper who once begged for food spent his Association stipend on fine shirts and griped about not being appreciated. He behaved with stunning entitlement and omniscience.

That arrogance came back to haunt him. Six months after Banks and the African Association hired him to chart Africa, America's first Nile explorer was hunkered down in a Cairo lavatory with a case of traveler's belly. He tried to treat it with a sulfurous substance known as vitriolic acid. Ledyard overdosed and began hemorrhaging. His death was miserable and humiliating, but quick. The British consul, recognizing that Ledyard was not English and was persona non grata with the Americans, hastily ordered him buried in an unmarked Cairo grave. He lies there still.

Joseph Banks had contingencies for just that situation. Even as he'd trumpeted Ledyard as the future of British exploration, he'd made a secondary hire, just in case. The African Association's other man was a courtier of King George III named Simon Lucas.

Ledyard's plan was to follow the Nile inland, then travel due west, to Timbuktu. Lucas's plan was to penetrate Africa by crossing the Sahara from north to south, then head east to the Nile.

Coincidentally, Lucas sallied forth just three weeks after Ledyard died. As a child, Barbary pirates had taken him prisoner. He endured years as a slave before being ransomed by the British. And while he had learned Arabic, and served as George III's Arab interpreter, Lucas didn't have an adventurous bone in his body. He quit his journey a few hundred miles after setting out, turning his camel around and racing north to the Mediterranean. The reasons he gave the African Association were thin, but his past traumas and political connections meant they didn't press him. All knew of Lucas's childhood, and his overwhelming fear of once again becoming the personal property of a Muslim warlord.

The subsequent expedition fared only slightly better. Daniel Houghton traveled so far into the Mali region of western Africa that he nearly laid eyes on the Niger before being robbed of all his belongings by Muslim slavers. Naked, starving, and lacking protective shelter, Houghton was torn apart by hyenas, then had his bones picked clean by vultures.

To say the least, the African Association was off to an inauspicious start. But Banks knew from personal experience that failures and setbacks are a vital part of exploration, bringing the goal one step closer each time.

8

Enter Lord Nelson. The vaunted British admiral destroyed Napoleon's navy at the Battle of the Nile in 1798, and the British established a toehold in northern Africa. The African Association no longer had the search for the source to themselves. Between 1798 and 1856 an eclectic collection of self-funded loners, thrill seekers, and adventurous aristocrats trekked upriver, chasing the source. Most were British. Some were Dutch. Or French. One, the young Belgian heiress Alexandrine Tinné, was female. Some followed the Nile inland from Cairo; others cut the tangent across East Africa. Most died from disease, animal attack, or murder. None found the source. The holy grail of exploration became more exalted as the failures mounted, like summiting Everest would become a century hence.

It was 1849 when a German adventurer named Johann Krapf first spotted snowcapped Mount Kenya in East Africa. A compatriot, Johannes Rebmann, discovered Mount Kilimanjaro, another nearby snowy peak. Both men were missionaries, and their discovery was soon published in a church magazine. However, the Royal Geographical Society in London quickly disparaged their findings, claiming that both peaks were in an equatorial region. And for snow to exist at the equator was clearly impossible.

And yet, if such mountains did actually exist, they might just be Ptolemy's legendary Mountains of the Moon.

Jack Speke cared little for the source, and even less for the Mountains of the Moon. Dick Burton was more interested in re-creating his Mecca adventure by sneaking into the African city of Harar, which had never before been infiltrated by a Christian. Both men would later claim that the source of the Nile was never far from their thoughts, but nothing could have been farther from the truth when Speke arrived in Aden in September 1854.

However, he was soon accepted as a member of Burton's expedition (comprised of Burton, Speke, army officer and surveyor G. E. Herne, naval officer and artist William Stroyan, and a complement of native gun bearers and porters). Finally, the British political agent, Colonel Outram, duly gave his permission for the group to enter Africa—this despite his serious misgivings about their safety.

On October 18, 1854, at 6:00 p.m., the group set sail for the Somali coast. The journey was supposed to take three days, but light winds and the Arab ship's captain's preference for anchoring at dusk and sailing only by daylight stretched the journey to nine. The grandeur of Africa was not immediately obvious to the British travelers when they finally reached the Somali coast, with their first port of Rakodah consisting of a small fort, several straw huts, and several other huts that had been burned to the ground by marauding tribes. And while Speke soon developed a taste for sour camel's milk, which he thought tasted "sharp and rough, like labourer's cider" and "the most delicious thing I ever drank," he was also somewhat disappointed by Africa. "I had now seen the Somali shore and must confess I was much disappointed," he wrote. "Hills and plains . . . were alike almost destitute of any vegetation; whilst not one animal or other living creature could be seen."

On the grand scale of things, the first Speke and Burton expedition was more of a minor probe than a grand journey. Upon getting settled in Somaliland, they split up and made cursory explorations of the interior. Burton reached Harar successfully,* and immersed himself in learning the chastity and sexual rituals of the locals, along with developing a fondness for an opiate called khat. Speke, meanwhile, shot gazelle and other small game while reconnoitering the countryside. At the end of the six months, the entire party returned to Aden to regroup.

At this point it was decided that they should attempt a more daring sort of exploration. What Burton had in mind was a journey inland to find the Mountains of the Moon, and the enduring fame that would come with finding the source of

---

*Though at great risk to his life. His Somali guides revealed his identity early in the journey, and he was forced to remove his native clothing and travel as a British officer. Burton was held prisoner by the local amir for ten days in Harar before being released.

the Nile. He did not imagine the journey as a lark, nor take it lightly. Burton was just curious about its precise location, and theorized that with enough guts and determination he would be the first man to see it in person. Speke, obviously, thought nothing of standing right next to Burton when this monumental moment came to pass.

This heightened level of curiosity is fascinating to behold.

Each of these men had put his life at great risk during their solitary forays into Somaliland. Many a man would have happily sailed home to London and regaled their friends forevermore with tales of their adventurous wanderings through unexplored Africa. There certainly would be no harm in that. But these men were motivated by different things—Stroyan, for instance, was a proponent of the burgeoning art of photography, which would have made him one of the first men to take a picture of the beauty of the African sunrise. Yet it is clear they let their considerable curiosity overwhelm any fear of danger or death.

It's unfortunate that Stroyan never got to photograph that sunrise, for it might have been a most memorable achievement. Instead, he was slaughtered on a Somali beach on the night of April 19, 1855, when a spear was thrust into his heart.

The night began quietly enough, with the expedition camped on the sand near Berbera. Dinner was served, and afterward, the men sat outside their tents drinking coffee and swapping stories, basking in the cool evening breeze blowing in off the Indian Ocean. It was almost idyllic in its setting, and the expedition was lulled into such a sense of security that they decided not to post sentries for the night.

"At the usual hour we all turned in to sleep," wrote Speke, "and silence reigned throughout the camp. A little after midnight, probably at one or two a.m., there suddenly arose a furious noise, as though the world were coming to an end. There was a terrible rush and hurry, then came sticks and stones, flying thick as hail, followed by a rapid discharge of firearms."

Some two hundred Somali tribesmen soon attacked the Burton Expedition's camp on the beach near Berbera, slashing at the canvas tents and killing men where they slept. Herne's pistol jammed early in the fighting, but he managed to flee down the beach to safety.

Neither Burton nor Speke was as lucky. As Burton swung his saber wildly at his attackers, a spear was thrust through his face. It passed from one side of his mouth and out the other cheek, knocking out two molars in the process. The fact that Burton managed to run down the beach with a very long spear sticking out both sides of his head is remarkable.

How Speke survived is much more like a miracle. His five-shot Adams pistol ran out of bullets quickly, and he was soon set upon by their attackers. "In another instant I was on the ground with a dozen Somali on the top of me. The man I had endeavoured to shoot wrenched the pistol out of my hand, and the way the scoundrel handled me sent a creeping shudder all over me. I felt as if my hair stood on end; and, not knowing who my opponents were, I feared that they belonged to a tribe called Eesa, who are notorious, not only for their ferocity in fighting, but for the unmanly mutilations they delight in," Speke wrote in his journal.

Speke was stripped and held captive all night long. His guard was a single thin Somali, who held tight to the rope binding Speke's wrists in front of his body. As morning dawned over the ocean, Speke had not yet been seriously hurt. On two occasions men had swung sabers at his torso, stopping the blades just an inch before they could slice into his flesh, then gleefully looking into the Englishman's eyes for signs of terror. Speke had also been threatened with death because his lack of circumcision clearly showed he was not a Muslim, but for a time that seemed to have been just a bluff.

Suddenly, everything changed.

"My jailer," wrote Speke in lucid detail, "who was still holding the string, stepped up close to me, and coolly stabbed me with his spear. I then raised my body a little in defence, when he knocked me down by jabbing his spear violently on my shoulder, almost cutting the jugular arteries. I rose again as he poised his spear, and caught the next prod, which was intended for my heart, on the back of one of my shackled hands; this gouged the flesh up to the bone. The cruel villain now stepped back a pace or two, to get me off my guard, and dashed his spear down to the bone of my left thigh. I seized it violently with both my hands, and would not relinquish the grip until he drew a shillelah from his girdle, and gave me such a violent blow on my left arm, I thought the bone was broken, and the spear fell helplessly from my hands. Finding his spear too blunt for running me through by a simple job when standing still, he now dropped the rope-end, walked back a dozen paces, and, rushing on me with savage fury, plunged his spear through the thick part of my right thigh into the ground, passing it between the thigh-bone and large sinew below."

In a final act of desperation, Speke struggled to his feet. "I sprang upon my legs and gave the miscreant such a sharp backhander in the face with my double bound fists that he lost his presence of mind," Speke wrote. Somehow, despite the spear wounds and blood loss and tied wrists, he then managed to sprint away from his jailer, dodging forty other Somalis and a number of hurled spears as he ran farther and farther down the beach. That the run continued for any length of time was due to the fact that Speke's attackers were losing interest in him and had begun looting the camp. Yet after almost four hours of torture and mutilation, his flight was by no means easy. Somehow, the naked explorer wandered more than three miles down the beach and linked up with his companions. In an even greater stroke of luck, a British mail ship was laying to just offshore. The camp having been deserted after the attack, a party was sent to retrieve Stroyan's mutilated body.*

The first Burton African expedition was over. Speke's

---

*The oppressive heat took its toll on Stroyan's corpse during the voyage back to Aden. It bloated and began to smell so badly that he was thrown overboard and buried at sea.

eleven wounds were so severe that he was given three years' convalescence by the army. Making matters worse, the beatings had inflicted bouts of temporary blindness.

Burton's palate and tongue were sliced, and he would bear a scar on his cheeks from the spear's entry wound for the rest of his life.

Unrelated to the attack, he was also suffering from syphilis.

The exploration careers of Jack Speke and Dick Burton appeared to be over as well. Burton was soon censured for the failed expedition, with its losses of lives and money, and no tangible success that might help the British gain a toehold in East Africa. Hoping to redeem himself, he returned to the army, where he saw service in the Crimean War, despite his disfigured face and difficulty in speaking.

Speke experienced a rather miraculous recovery, and soon found himself serving on the front lines in Turkey as well. When the Crimean War ended, he tramped about the Asian subcontinent once again, back to his familiar ritual of hunting and collecting plants.

Problem was, Dick Burton and Jack Speke's curiosity was still very much alive. The sharp stab of spears impaling their bodies and the smell of a dead and rotting friend did nothing to lessen that drive. And while an unscathed G. E. Herne never entered the annals of exploration again, Burton and Speke were soon dreaming anew of finding the source of the

Nile—though they had made such a mess of things that it was clear their chances of receiving the funding or permissions for a second chance were almost nonexistent.

Curiosity was no longer enough. Now they also needed something stronger to get them to the next leg of their journey.

Something stronger called hope.

HOPE

Shall I abandon, O King of mysteries, the soft comforts of home?

Shall I turn my back on my native land, and turn my face towards the sea?

Shall I put myself wholly at Your mercy, without silver, without a horse, without fame, without honor?

Shall I throw myself wholly upon You, without sword and shield, without food and drink, without a bed to lie on?

Shall I say farewell to my beautiful land, placing myself under Your yoke?

Shall I pour out my heart to You, confessing my manifold sins and begging forgiveness, tears streaming down my cheeks?

Shall I leave the prints of my knees on the sandy beach, a record of my final prayer in my native land?

Shall I then suffer every kind of wound that the sea can inflict?

Shall I take my tiny boat across the wide sparkling ocean?

O *King of the Glorious Heaven, shall I go of my own choice*
  upon the sea?
O *Christ, will You help me on the wild waves?*
                    —Prayer of St. Brendan the Navigator

1

Imagine a world without exploration. Try to comprehend a time when people lived their entire lives without traveling from one valley to the next, let alone sailing across oceans with no visible end. This is what life is like on the western coast of Ireland in roughly AD 530, more than a thousand years before Christopher Columbus sets sail from the port of Cadiz en route to what will come to be known as the New World. An Irish monk named Brendan is about to undertake a most extraordinary adventure. In a time where little is known about navigation, or the height and depth and breadth of the oceans, he has built a very small boat known as a curragh. The construction is rather crude, with a hull made of interwoven twigs, reeds, and branches. This was covered in ox hides tanned in oak bark and then softened with butter. A sail and mast were rigged. Once skins were laid atop the 36-foot-long open boat to provide shelter from the elements, Brendan and a dozen other monks set forth from what is now Dingle Bay. He has just fasted for forty days and nights to clear his head for the arduous journey to come, which makes him perhaps the first man in exploration history to undertake the deprivation and hardship of an expedition before actually leaving home.

What Brendan hopes to find is a mythical land of milk and honey; a heaven on Earth, and a "land of promise and of the saints." The reasons are unclear. He doesn't appear to be driven by the need to proselytize or colonize. Money is not an issue, for as a monk Brendan's life is one of self-chosen poverty. But for some reason, at the ripe old age of forty-four, Brendan has gotten tired of looking out over the horizon and wondering whether this legendary paradise exists. So he is going to do something about it.

2

As long as there have been oceans, men have longed to know what lies on the other side—or if there is another side. The ancient age of nautical exploration was led by the Greeks and Egyptians, who plied the Mediterranean and Indian Oceans. The Ancients were the first explorers to introduce mapmaking and travel writing, marking the first permanent records of exploration. One of the earliest recorded expeditions was led by the Egyptian nobleman Hannu. In 2750 BC he sailed a ship down the length of the Red Sea to the tip of the Arabian Peninsula. What he hoped to find is unclear, because when he got to his destination he had landed at none other than what would one day be called Aden, that dusty volcanic hellhole Burton and Speke would label "the Devil's Punchbowl."

In 600 BC the Egyptian pharaoh Necho funded a three-year expedition that reportedly circumnavigated the coast of Africa. This beat Portuguese discoverer Vasco da Gama by two thousand years, and took place a full millennium before Brendan began his prevoyage fast.

But what made Brendan's voyage unique, separating him from the three thousand years of sailors that preceded him, was that he aimed his curragh straight out into the ocean rather than sailing within sight of the coast. It was the nautical equivalent of stepping off the edge of a cliff. With that simple act of turning mere curiosity into the hope that his actions would result in a discovery, Brendan began exploration's nautical era.

It was an epoch that would not end until the death of James Cook thirteen centuries later, whereupon it was universally agreed that, with the exception of the odd archipelago, the oceans had all been completely charted. Mankind thereupon focused almost completely on land-based exploration and solving great geographical mysteries, such as finding the source of the Nile River.

A book detailing the oral history of Brendan's seven-year odyssey, *The Voyage of Saint Brendan the Abbot*, published nearly a thousand years after he set sail, recounts his discoveries of such oddities as icebergs, walrus, Eskimos, and even the fiery volcanoes of what we now call Iceland. He island-hopped across the Atlantic on a circuitous path that also took him to North America, and then back home via the Azores. It is said that in his younger days as an up-and-coming sailor, Christopher Columbus passed through western Ireland and visited the Dingle Peninsula in search of information about Brendan's voyage. Whether this is true is unclear. What is for sure, however, is that Columbus owned a copy of *The Voyage of Saint Brendan the Abbot* (in Latin: *Navigatio Sancti Brendani Abatis*) and was a believer in a mythical island in the Atlantic named for the monk, which appeared on many nautical maps in the Middle Ages.

It has been suggested by the eminent historian Barbara Tuchman that Columbus's four voyages of discovery were so revolutionary that the common man shifted his worldview from "the hereafter to the here and now," setting aside the Catholic Church's orthodox view of a known and finite world in favor of a vast, unknown planet whose mysteries would be revealed by those intrepid and curious enough to go looking. This not only led to the Age of Enlightenment, with its deep thirst for knowledge,* but also to that schism in the Church known as the Reformation.

So it's ironic that this upheaval began with a very pious Catholic adventurer. The hope Brendan had in finding an earthly paradise was transferred, over the centuries, to Columbus, and also to the countless navigators in the thirteen-

---

*A new creation known as the coffeehouse was vital to this era. They sprang up in Britain and quickly became hubs of intellectual debate. The appeal lay in their availability to individuals of all income levels because the cost of participation was a single cup of coffee. This allowed the uneducated to listen in and learn as great ideas were tossed back and forth in a casual setting.

hundred-year span ranging from Brendan to Cook who endured the unpredictable terrors and delights of life at sea.

Strangely, this hope deserted Brendan in his final hours. He died in 577 while visiting his sister, Briga, the abbess of a convent some distance from Dingle Bay. The ninety-one-year-old Brendan was terrified of what lay beyond the grave. "I fear the unknown land, the presence of my King and the sentence of my judge," he told Briga with his dying breath. Though not normally words associated with a man of deep faith, they suggest that the staggering natural wonders like waterspouts and gale-force winds and mighty waves twice the size of a house he had seen during his journeys had left a deep impression on his imagination. If that sort of thing existed on Earth, what sort of hell awaited him if his day of judgment went poorly?

Or perhaps it was the lack of a goal. The connection between hope and a longed-for outcome is paramount. Among explorers, belief in themselves and their mission was pandemic. Though many possessed stoic dispositions, or were unable to express their emotions in the sort of upbeat manner that so often corresponds with optimism, the journals of explorers are shining examples of hope and optimism against long odds: Henry Morton Stanley's belief that he was destined to find David Livingstone, who had been lost in Africa for more than five years and was presumed dead; Ernest Shackleton's conviction that his improbable open-boat journey across the Southern Ocean would lead him and his men to safety; and Charles Lindbergh's apparent fearlessness upon taking off for Paris, despite the fact that he was attempting to become the first man to fly solo across the Atlantic Ocean.

Without hope, of course, there is little sense undertaking an expedition. But to summon hope daily, even when there seems no point in going on, was one of the explorer's most engaging qualities. To give up hope was to quit, and that was not an option. It was hope that led Robert Peary to repeatedly battle the Arctic, even when others began to perceive him as a fool. "I tried to realize," he wrote of his success after finally reaching the North Pole, "that after twenty-three years of struggles and discouragement I had at last succeeded in placing the flag of my country at the goal of the world's desire."

Hope is not just a happy feeling. It is a dynamic cognitive emotional system that is markedly different from mere optimism. When an individual dreams (or daydreams, as is more often the case) of some ultimate goal they would like to achieve, the process of hope uses creative intelligence and the intricate workings of the brain to find a road map toward the eventual completion of that goal. Goals fostered by hope are what are known as learning goals, which psychologists attribute to success and fulfillment in many areas of life, thanks to their focus on strategies to attain these goals.

3

Consider the fourth voyage of Christopher Columbus. His first, and most famous, journey in 1492 had seen him discover the New World. He had been trying to reach Asia by sailing west across "the Ocean Sea" to help Spain capture the market in pepper, silk, and opiates. It had been decreed by the pope that rival nation Portugal controlled the coast of Africa and all routes eastward to the Orient. For this reason Portugal would soon dominate trade on that continent for centuries to come—particularly slavery. The path Burton and Speke followed in their search for the source was the same trail Arab slavers used to march newly captured slaves to Portuguese traders on the coast.

Columbus was obsessed with the goal of finding that westward route to Asia, for it would enrich not only his Spanish patrons, but himself as well. For a man born into the middle class, exploration represented a chance at wealth and nobility. This is important, because outside of sailing, Columbus had no other marketable skills. He was a nominal cartographer and a poor businessman who had a deep fondness for powerful women. "The Admiral of the Ocean Sea," as he would one day be known, stood roughly six feet tall, had red hair, and a fair, perhaps even freckled, complexion. No one knows for sure, because he never once had his image painted or drawn.

In 1492 he discovered the New World. In 1493 he undertook a second voyage, to colonize his new empire (Columbus's agreement with the Spanish crown gave him control of much of the New World's land and wealth), while also continuing to search for that elusive path to Asia. By 1498 the colonists were disenchanted with their new lives and Columbus returned in an attempt to bring about order. Once again, he used this voyage to find the Orient. He failed, but did manage to stumble upon South America.

The third voyage ended badly. The Spanish crown had him thrown in chains and returned to Spain. He was almost fifty years old by then, a decade beyond the average life expectancy of the time. His hair was gray and his hands were shriveled from rheumatoid arthritis. And when he asked Queen Isabella, the biggest advocate of his adventures, for a royal audience, she refused.

But then she changed her mind. Columbus literally got down on his knees to beg for one more chance to find that path to Asia.

Isabella could be aloof and distant. She was a very small woman who wielded power brilliantly, and was the equal of any man when it came to planning war or running a government. But she was not insensitive to Columbus's pleas. Though a very devout Catholic (so pious, in fact, that she refused to bathe because it was considered licentious), she seems to have had a thing for the tall, rugged sailor. There is no evidence that there was an improper relationship between them, but for more than a decade there had been a flirtation. Now, seated in her throne room at the Alhambra with her husband, Ferdinand, she took pity on Columbus and granted him one last voyage.

What a voyage it was. He set sail from Spain on May 11, 1502. In short order, Columbus raced to Africa to intervene in a military dispute with the Moors, predicted a hurricane as he finally reached the New World, was ignored when he attempted to warn the colonists at Hispaniola (modern-day Dominican Republic and Haiti), and successfully found shelter from the storm, even as twenty-nine of the thirty ships in port at Hispaniola were destroyed, along with five hundred lives.

And this was just the first two months of the trip. Before the journey ended two years later, Columbus endured shark attacks, warfare with local tribes, mutiny, waterspouts, the loss of one of his three ships, an infestation of shipworms, predicted a lunar eclipse that saved the lives of him and his men, and for one long year on Jamaica, shipwreck. As all this was going on, he also suffered from gout and a temporary blindness known as ophthalmia, which came about from staring too long at the sun-drenched sea.

The fourth (or "El Alte Viaje"—the high voyage, as Columbus considered it his best work) was a journey where anything that could go wrong, did go wrong. Yet Columbus never stopped looking for that path to Asia. Driven by hope, he pressed on, even as those shipworms were making his vessels so porous that the hulls were filling with seawater. Like Brendan and Cook, those other two tent poles of nautical exploration, Columbus did not undertake his discoveries in a linear, point-to-point, fashion.* Instead, he wandered back and forth across the seas like a bloodhound stalking a scent, sailing this way and

---

*This is a hallmark of all great explorers. The only exceptions to that rule are polar, mountaineering, and space exploration, for which wandering is not an option due to refueling and gravitational concerns.

that in search of new peoples, lands, rivers, and oceans. Hardships and setbacks may have been nuisances, but they were also expected facts of life if dreams were to become reality.

Big dreams die hard, but on Christmas Day 1502 Columbus let the discovery of Asia slip away. With that, his exploration career effectively came to an end. Beaten down by setbacks and painful inflictions, Columbus anchored in a small protective harbor and gave up his quest. He then careened his ships up onto the beach and spent a week repairing them for the long journey back to Spain.

If only he had known how close he was to seeing that dream come true. The Pacific Ocean, and its direct route to Asia, lay just a thirty-five-mile march through the jungle, for Columbus had inadvertently and quite miraculously dropped anchor at what is now the mouth of the Panama Canal. By sending his men overland, Columbus could have become the first European to find the Pacific.* But the great admiral had no way of knowing this. Instead, stripped of all hope, he weighed anchor and began his trip home. Columbus arrived in Spain just in time to see his beloved Queen Isabella on her deathbed, but Ferdinand denied him the opportunity to visit with her one last time.

---

*That honor would fall to Vasco Núñez de Balboa ten years later. Balboa, who took up exploration after being inspired by Columbus's journeys, later fell victim to political intrigue and was beheaded by Spanish officials in the New World. It is said that it took the executioner three swings of the ax to sever his head.

Mapmakers would name the New World after Amerigo Vespucci, a banker with a flair for self-promotion, who wrote widely read published accounts of his time as a passenger on two voyages to what became known as the Americas.*

Columbus died two years after Isabella, in 1506, at age fifty-four, whereupon Spanish politics contrived to have his voyages written out of the history books for the next three centuries. Much attention has been placed on Columbus's discovery of the New World, and how it changed the course of civilization. His New World exploded into a land of great cities and the flourishing of ideals such as democracy. Explorers crossed from east to west and north to south, charting its interior. Roads were built. The New World's advances were breathtaking.

Yet Columbus was considered a failure in his day. His discoveries did not yield the gold, spices, or slaves for which the Spanish sovereigns longed. It was Portuguese navigators such as Da Gama and Dias who were lauded for the manner in which their great successes enriched the country's throne.

And they did it by finding a way to chart, and then plunder, the continent of Africa—in particular, the areas south of the impassable Sahara Desert.

Their solution was to approach central Africa by sea.

*This same Latinizing of a name would eventually swing Columbus's way. The District of Columbia, the Columbia River, Columbia University, and the nation of Colombia all get their names from Columbus.

4

Somewhat problematically, there was nothing inviting about this portion of Africa. Danger was, literally, everywhere. Half of all white men died within two years of setting foot on the continent. Almost every native tribe was hostile. The animals weren't just large, they were enormous, prehistoric, and terrifying—lions, crocodiles, elephants, hippopotamuses—the like of which Europeans had never seen before. Dozens of varieties of poisonous snakes slithered through the thick jungles and across the grassy plains. The equatorial temperatures were unbearably hot. Malaria, sleeping sickness, and other equatorial parasites killed more men than all those other dangers combined. And the weather was so fierce it became synonymous with Africa itself—the term "dark continent" had many meanings, but one of them referred to how the sky could turn pitch black at noon when a storm drenched the horizon.

As other nations began to develop a nautical ability on par with that of the Portuguese, and to thumb their nose at the Treaty of Tordesillas,* the Portuguese were suddenly forced to share eastern Africa.

The English, as all of this was happening, stayed home.

---

*A pact splitting the known world into two spheres of influence, one controlled by Portugal and the other by Spain. It was brokered by a pre-Reformation pope in 1494, and meant little to nations no longer in lockstep with Rome.

Their seafaring abilities were limited to trips across the English Channel and North Sea. Until the seventeenth century, the term "British explorer" was an oxymoron. Those English navigators who stumbled into exploration, à la Sir Francis Drake and William Dampier, did so as a by-product of piracy. Britain was an island nation and content to stay that way.*

Then in 1688, William of Orange ascended to the throne, bringing with him the vaunted power of the Dutch navy. From then on, Britain became obsessed with colonizing the world to exploit its wealth (colonies provided raw goods for British manufacturers, whose products could then be exported).

Thus Britain, over the next one hundred years, became a nation of explorers—nautical explorers. The pinnacle of this era were Cook's voyages, which commingled with the Age of Reason to shrink the globe and make mankind want to know more about it. By 1788 the British capital had followed in the footsteps of Rome, Beijing, Seville, and, for a flicker, Lisbon,

---

*The explorer Sebastian Cabot made several voyages to the New World for England in the late 1490s and early 1500s. A Venetian by birth (real name: Sebastiano Caboto), he shifted his allegiance to Spain during the reign of Henry VIII due to their greater emphasis on exploration. It's worth noting that the actor Sebastian Cabot, who rose to fame as the beloved Mr. French on the television show *Family Affair* in the late 1960s, was born with that name and did not borrow it from the famous explorer. The same can also be said for the Welsh actor Richard Walter Jenkins. The twelfth son of a hard-drinking coal miner, he adopted the last name of Burton to honor a beloved schoolmaster—not, as it is easy to assume, as an attempt to co-opt the swaggering reputation of the explorer Richard Burton.

to become that era's hub of global discovery. "London," as the *Times* proudly noted of the Earth's largest city, "is the emporium of all the world and the wonder of foreigners."

Nevertheless, it was Columbus who reduced the somewhat dazzling concept of sailing across the ocean into a common occurrence. Before we leave him, it's important to note that while Columbus was brimming with hope on each and every one of his voyages, he was also a decided pessimist. This would seem like cognitive dissonance, but in fact hope and optimism are two very different things. Hope begins with a dream, turns that dream into a goal, and mentally comes up with a solution to see that dream come true.

Optimism, on the other hand, is merely a belief that everything's going to be okay. There's no plan or attention to detail that will make this sentiment a reality. People with hope tend to have a powerful belief that they control their destiny. Optimists, on the other hand, tend to set what are known as mastery goals, which are easily attainable, and depend upon sheer willpower and happy thoughts. Too often, however, that willpower fades when the goal becomes harder and harder to attain. Frustration sets in. The individual quits. This leads to a sort of learned helplessness, where individuals feel that they are powerless over their future. Despair follows.

On the other hand, those who possess hope have the ability to tap into "divergent thinking"—which is essentially the brain's ability to let random thoughts ricochet around, using every single bit of knowledge it contains to find an optimal outcome. Hope, one 1997 study showed, was a greater indicator of success than "training, self-esteem, confidence, and mood."*

5

In 1735, during a French expedition to the equatorial region of South America's Andes mountain range, explorer Charles Marie de La Condamine employed a surveyor named Jean Godin to make scientific measurements. History does not record whether Godin was very selective, extremely lonely, or merely unattractive. At any rate, he was a thirty-five-year-old man who soon fell in love with a mere child. Isabel Grameson was the fourteen-year-old daughter of a local administrator— and Godin's bride, as of two days after Christmas in 1741. Isabel was beautiful, but her family was also very wealthy, which might have enhanced the attraction. At any rate, the unlikely couple soon began a family and lived together happily for eight years. But in March of 1749, Godin received news from France that his father had died. He decided it was time to return home, and bring his family with him. Godin then undertook the rather extraordinary feat of traveling all the way from one side of South America to the other—literally, the length of the Amazon River—to his nation's nearest dip-

*"Hope and Academic Success in College." Research done at the University of Kansas. Work published in the *Journal of Educational Psychology* 94, no. 4 (2002): 820–26.

lomatic outpost in French Guiana to acquire the necessary permissions.

There was, however, a problem: Spain and Portugal were at odds with France. So when Godin tried to travel back upriver to Ecuador, Portuguese officials in Brazil denied him permission to reenter the Amazon basin. Traveling around to the other side of South America via sailing ship was also out of the question, because, as a Frenchman, he would be denied entry into Ecuador by the Spanish authorities controlling that country.

So Godin did the only thing he could do: wait. He became a resident of French Guiana, and for years and years, scanned the horizon each morning for the arrival of his wife, knowing that she would arrive eventually. In 1765, after more than fifteen long years, Portuguese officials relented. It was arranged that a boat would travel up the Amazon to fetch Godin's beloved Isabel. This, in itself, was an epic journey. To make matters more arduous, Isabel would have to travel up and over the Andes, one of the world's premier mountain ranges, to meet the ship at the Amazon's headwaters.

Isabel was nearly forty by then. She hadn't seen her husband in two decades. All but one of their children had died of smallpox. Ignoring those in her village who suggested she was undertaking a suicide mission, Isabel walked off to meet her husband.

At first, Isabel was not alone. When she left the village of Riobamba at the end of 1769 she traveled with her grown son Joachim, her two brothers, a nephew, thirty-one Indians, three servants, and three traveling Frenchmen. From Riobamba they traveled to Canelos, a mission station at the head of the Bobonaza River. It took them seven days to travel the 60 miles, during which time a smallpox virus devastated Isabel's fellow travelers. Just a handful remained alive when Isabel and the remaining group pressed on down the Bobonaza in dugout canoes. One of the Frenchmen soon fell overboard and drowned. Another, thinking their plight hopeless, elected to go ahead alone and return with help. He never came back.

After four weeks, Isabel's dwindling expedition numbered just seven. They were out of food and their canoes had rotted. She constructed a raft from native trees and set off again, but the raft hit a submerged obstacle almost immediately and fell apart. Another member of her expedition died of fever that night, followed by two more the next. One woman wandered off into the forest, never to be seen again. Isabel's two brothers and her nephew died. Then Isabel herself was laid low by sickness. She slipped into an unconscious state for two days. When she woke up, dead bodies were all around her in the jungle. Isabel was alone. She had no means of transportation, no food, and no supplies. But she was alive, and determined to see her husband once again.

After wandering alone in the rain forest for nine days, she encountered two Indians who took her to the mission station in Andoas. When they arrived she rewarded them with the two gold necklaces she had been wearing. But the mission's two priests confiscated the necklaces, saying the Indians were unworthy of such wealth. An incensed Isabel set off alone from the mission immediately, ignoring the priests' demands that she stop. She was naked, save for "the soles of the shoes of her dead brothers."

Isabel walked along the muddy banks until she reached another mission. There the priests offered to pay for her to return to Riobamba, a suggestion so appalling that she immediately set out again. Finally Isabel reached the waiting ship and traveled down the Amazon to be with her husband. In all, she journeyed 3,000 miles over the course of ten months before finally wrapping her arms around Jean. "After twenty years absence and a long endurance, I again met with a cherished wife who I had almost given up every hope of seeing again," he wrote of that day.

But Jean didn't give up hope, and neither did Isabel. Their story would not be possible without it. Isabel's adventure down the Amazon was etched so indelibly in her soul that to her dying day, she refused to enter the woods ever again. Luckily for her, that dying day took place in France, twenty-two very happy years after leaving the Amazon behind. She outlived her husband by just six months.

6

From Brendan to Columbus to the Portuguese to Isabel Godin, the lineage of exploration and success in the face of impossible odds was marked by an abiding belief in the power of hope. And so as the next link in that centuries-long chain of men and women who earned the title of explorer, Jack Speke and Dick Burton were also consumed with a sense of hope as they pondered a return to Africa.

As the Crimean War wound down, separately, and unbeknownst to one another, Speke and Burton were longing to venture back into the continent that had almost killed them. Some two years after the debacle on the beach in Somaliland, his wounds now nothing more than rather gruesome scars, Speke was telling friends that he "was dying to go back and try again." This appeared to be a lost cause, because he wasn't fluent in Arabic or any of the native languages (nor any but his mother tongue), lacked credibility as an explorer due to the Somaliland failure, and, because he had never attended university, lacked the education to qualify as a scientific observer of any new discoveries.

Burton was highly qualified to return, but his handicaps were far more profound and of his own making. As leader of the previous expedition, its public failure—which included the gruesome death of an English gentleman—was deemed his responsibility. Electing to fight in the Crimean War was a means of getting out of London long enough for the pressure to die down and for things to be forgotten. Having this absence correspond with military service added elements of patriotism and heroism, which helped Burton's public image. Even more so, *Pilgrimage to El-Medinah and Meccah*, Burton's book about his daring adventure into Mecca, had finally hit British bookstores in early 1855, adding to his growing legend. Put all three of those together—military service, time away from London, and fame as a risk-taking explorer—and Burton was soon finalizing plans to take another shot at finding the source.

Which begs the question: Why the Nile? Why not the Amazon or the Mississippi?* Burton and Speke would have found plenty of adventure on either of those mighty rivers. The same combination of hostile indigenous peoples, terrifying snakes and mammals, and deprivations incumbent with a plunge into the vast unknown awaited them there as well.

The answer is twofold. The first is practical, having to do with Britain's desire to exploit a continent within their frame of reference. Portugal controlled the Amazon, and the United States was in the process of sending thousands of families across the Great Plains on the Oregon Trail, effectively cementing sea-to-shining-sea control of almost all the North American landmass. Britain might succeed in sending explorers up the Amazon and the Mississippi, but little short of a military invasion would have allowed them to harvest any natural resources for British use.

Not so with the Nile. The interior of Africa was still wide open to exploration and exploitation.

The second reason for choosing the Nile is far less practical. That reason was immortality.

---

*The Nile is the longest river in the world, the Amazon is number two, and the Mississippi is number four. At the time, the British were unaware that China's Yangtze would have nestled into the third position.

Not even the great empires of Egypt, Greece, or Rome were able to find the source, despite centuries of theorizing and countless failed attempts. And Britain, which fancied itself an empire every bit the equal of those three, considered this just one more achievement that would prove it.

Broken down to its essence, finding the source is simply a search for water—two hydrogen molecules bonding with a single oxygen molecule in the bowels of the Earth, then seeping forth somewhere in the heart of Africa. The water becomes a trickle, then a stream, then a mighty river—the longest on Earth, rolling effortlessly from mountains through jungle through the Sahara through Cairo and into the Mediterranean. The river takes its name from the Egyptian *nelios*, meaning "river valley." Mankind's most prolific kingdoms have risen and fallen on its verdant shores. Moses, Julius Caesar, and Napoleon drank her waters. The Nile never shrivels, despite not having tributaries, substantial rainfall, or other obvious means of replenishment. She even floods during September, the hottest month of the year in northern Africa. Farmers plant their crops in her fertile silt once the floodwaters recede. Lush green fields blossom in the desert as if the Nile is life itself.

Theories about the source's location ranged from the equator to the bottom of the world—or maybe an even greater river, fed by an ocean, that slices like an aqueduct across the entire African continent. In 460 BC, Herodotus, the Greek "father of history," took it upon himself to find out.

Herodotus imagined enormous fountains spewing the Nile

geyser-like from the Earth, and set off alone to witness the spume and mist. But 600 miles inland from Cairo, the languid brown snake turned white at the waterfalls that would some-day become known as the First Cataract. Like sentinels, they guarded the Nile's inner reaches. The desert turned to jungle and swamp. The civilized world ended and a land of cannibals began. Herodotus turned back.

The mystery was still unanswered when Ptolemy drew the first conclusive world map in AD 140. Basing his speculation on African legend, he said that the source lay in snow-covered peaks along the equator, which he dubbed "the Mountains of the Moon." Critics wrongly ridiculed that idea, saying that snow couldn't possibly exist in equatorial latitudes. Neither Ptolemy nor those critics traveled up the Nile to see if he was right. The source's mystery and mystique eventually became legend. The source became a force unto itself, too great for man to divine or witness. "It is not given to us mortals," the French author Montesquieu wrote in the eighteenth century, "to see the Nile feeble and at its source."

Centuries passed. Global exploration turned away from Africa. The reason was simple geography: it is almost impos-sible to travel from northern Africa to central Africa on land. The endless sands of the Sahara Desert are part of the reason. The other is the Nile itself. Soon after the First Cataract, it slows to a quagmire known as the Sudd, an impenetrable morass of water hyacinths and papyrus that stretches for hundreds of miles. The dense swamp is home to crocodiles, hippopotamuses, thick black clouds of mosquitoes, and the 400-pound Nile perch. Half of all water flowing into the Sudd evaporates into the atmosphere, thanks to the steamy equatorial heat. Which is why the roaring Nile, after 3,000 free-flowing, undisturbed miles, slows to a near halt.

The casual traveler didn't stand a chance against the Sahara, and even less of a chance against the Sudd. A vast migration of cultures was unthinkable. In this way, Egypt prospered and advanced the course of civilization, benefiting from the exchange of ideas that occurred through constant communication, warring, and intermarrying with other peoples in northern Africa and the Mediterranean Rim.

Thanks to this cruel geography, the tribes of Africa living south of the Sudd did not take part in this advance. The land and their people stayed the same as they had for centuries before: a cultural island and a mystery to the outside world for thousands of years after Alexander the Great conquered the Egyptians.

This was the land that Burton and Speke prepared to enter.

7

By sheer coincidence, James Erhardt and Johann Rebmann, the German missionaries who claimed to have seen the Mountains of the Moon a few years earlier, sent a brand-new map home to their employers at the Church Missionary Society at almost precisely the same moment in history. Basing their drawing on descriptions provided by Arab slave traders, they portrayed a network of lakes in central Africa that might provide a clue to the location of the source. The CMS, not being in the exploration business, passed it on to the proper British authority, the Royal Geographical Society.

Begun in 1830 as a British adjunct to similar societies in Paris and Berlin, the London Geographical Society's mission was to advance the knowledge of geography. With King William IV as its patron, the London Geographical Society became the Royal Geographical Society, soon overtaking Paris and Berlin to become the leading body in its field.

And since the advancement of geographical knowledge is most easily accomplished through global exploration, this also became their domain. Sir Joseph Banks had died ten years earlier, but he would have been happy to know that his African Association would be absorbed by the RGS, and his dream of finding the source carried on by another generation.

The Royal Geographical Society discussed the Erhardt/Rebmann findings during their winter meetings in late 1855. It was widely agreed that although the map may have been inaccurate in their estimation—this notion being based on the previous writings of Ptolemy, Herodotus, and other classical works on Africa—it certainly represented a new key to finding the source. Soon there was talk about sending a new expedition to verify this information.

As all this was taking place, Dick Burton returned home

from the Crimea. It was only a matter of time before he heard about Erhardt and Rebmann's map.

But before Burton could seriously ponder a return to Africa, he had to deal with a very public cloud of shame now swirling about him. His commanding officer in the Crimea had been W. F. Beatson, a make-up-your-own-rules general cut from the same cloth as Burton, who had spent the better part of his career in India. Beatson had been forced to resign his command during the war amid charges from rivals within the British military that he could not control his troops. Beatson filed suit against his enemies for defamation of character upon his return to London. In an example of putting out the fire with gasoline, Beatson chose the ever-controversial Burton to testify in his behalf.

Burton proceeded to talk down to the court in a grand and rather sarcastic manner, using his superior intellect to mock the opposing attorneys. Even though Burton's efforts led to Beatson's vindication, his public behavior led to a revenge-driven series of rumors that had the effect of greatly assassinating Burton's character. Chief among these were begun by a fellow officer, who began circulating sordid rumors, including the fabrication that Burton had been caught in a Turkish harem and castrated. These tales might have been ignored if there weren't at least a little truth in them. Burton's fondness for the prurient and pornographic was an open secret. Those who heard the gossip were at the very least titillated—and at the most, appalled. "Pious mothers loathed Burton's name," wrote Burton biographer Thomas Wright in 1906. "And even men of the world mentioned it apologetically."

It's a wonder that any respectable woman would have looked twice at Burton during that time, considering the damage it might do to her own good name. But in the midst of the controversy, Burton began courting Isabel Arundel, the beautiful and devout Catholic woman he would one day marry. Her mother, having heard the rumors, was appalled. "He is not an old English," she told Isabel, warning her daughter to stay away. "He is not a Catholic. He has neither money nor prospects."

Soon Burton would have both. For despite the controversy and innuendo, Burton was still very much an explorer. He approached the Royal Geographic Society about a journey into central Africa to verify Erhardt and Rebmann's mysterious map.

Now, the leadership of the RGS was not the band of swashbuckling adventurers one might expect to be leading a society devoted to death-defying exploration. Its members included politicians, linguists, scientists, orientalists, merchants, engineers, cartographers, ethnographers, and a great number of wealthy gentlemen who enjoyed dabbling in arts and knowledge.

These were respectable men, living in Victorian London at a time when decorum and propriety were of the utmost importance. Very few were actively adventurous. They were led by Sir Roderick Murchison, a Scot who had been on the verge of squandering his inheritance when his wife urged him to take up a hobby more respectable than drinking and fox hunting. He chose geology, and became an expert in the field. Murchison's 1839 opus *The Silurian System* categorized Paleozoic marine invertebrate fossils in the Welsh border regions, and was named for a British tribe in that region that had successfully resisted Roman invasion. The book earned him worldwide respect and acclaim.

In addition to being a scholar, Murchison was also very much a showman. One famous photo shows him arriving at a geological dig wearing white top hat and tails.

The combination of these two traits would make the RGS great. It was Murchison whose genius elevated its public celebrity above the British Association for the Advancement of Science, the Geological Society, and any of a number of other societies then existent in London to expand mankind's knowledge of the universe. He served as its president and chief apologist off and on from 1843 to 1871, and oversaw the RGS's evolution from a curious group of travelers who wanted to know more about the world, into nothing less than the body most responsible for the expansion of the British Empire. Every time an explorer entered a new land and claimed it for England, Queen Victoria's stake in the world got a little bigger. No wonder that Murchison has been nicknamed "the Architect of Empire."

The RGS medal, bestowed annually, became the symbol of greatness in exploration achievement. Murchison made the charting of Africa and the discovery of the Nile's source his greatest priorities. Even as British explorers were venturing into Asia, South America, and Canada, Murchison held his African explorers in the highest esteem. They were his "lions," and he did all in his power to ensure that their achievements were trumpeted in the newspapers and that their published journals became best sellers. Murchison was not the first man to realize there was great wealth and fame in being an explorer, yet no other man had exploited it so ruthlessly for personal gain.

Not everyone could be a lion. Murchison made sure that only the most qualified individuals received RGS funding. David Livingstone, for instance, became so famous after his journeys that he was not only mobbed on the streets of London, he was also mobbed when he attended church.

What separated Burton and Murchison—one an explorer and the other an exploration cheerleader—was their source of hope. Burton was driven by curiosity and a deep desire to push his personal limits by exploring deeper into Africa. Murchison was equally curious about the unknown spots on the map, but his dreams were much more limited. The man who fostered the British Empire was reluctant to leave the comforts of England for the sacrifice of exploration.

The white top hat and tails had no place in Africa.

8

Murchison was a social animal, and befriended many of the great explorers of his day to bask in their reflected glory. Yet he would always remain distant from Burton and his constant whiff of scandal. Nonetheless, Murchison recognized a bold opportunity when he saw one. And the plan that Burton presented to the RGS in the early months of 1856 was both elaborate and intensely researched. For his dream of venturing into Africa to become a reality, Burton was well aware that he had to present himself as the ultimate professional. This was Burton's last chance. He may have succeeded in Mecca, but that achievement was three long years ago. The list of embarrassments, setbacks, and outright failures since then would have doomed a less ambitious man. One more would surely disgrace Burton and spell the end of official governmental permissions—and private funding—for his adventures.

That scar on his cheek only made matters worse. It was like a scarlet letter, reminding one and all of his Somaliland failure, and reinforcing the notion that the man standing before them was the reprobate Burton. The scar had been such an emblem of bad behavior that it originally kept Burton out of the Crimean War. He had literally traveled from regiment to regiment when he first arrived in the Crimea, looking for a unit that would offer him a commission. Each time he was refused. His eventual posting was only made possible because the unit was comprised of Turkish irregulars, and the irascible General Beatson was desperate for any officer who possessed the stones to train them.

The scar would one day become a source of pride. As Burton got older and heavier, the scar traveled from his cheek up closer to his eyes—yet it never faded away. And while he was deeply nervous about appearing unattractive when Frederic

Leighton painted his portrait in 1872, Burton chose to appear in profile, revealing the scarred side of his face like the badge of honor it had become.

Sixteen years earlier, however, driven by the hope of one last grand act of redemption, Burton pored over every sort of material relating to central Africa he could find: theories passed down for almost two thousand years, old maps, legends, and the accounts of French, British, Dutch, and Portuguese travelers. He determined that the journey's destination should be a place called Ujiji, on the shores of this hypothetical lake Erhardt and Rebmann's map portrayed, and that they should follow Arab slaving trails.

Burton did not specifically mention a search for the source. For purposes of funding the mission, it was much better to focus his travels on potential commercial exploitation. But the Nile was never far from Burton's planning. The "Unveiling of Isis,*" as he liked to call it, was just the sort of grand achievement that would end his public disgrace.

And then he went one step farther, in an act that reveals some of the ingenious problem solving in which the brain engages when it comes to hope: Burton, the ultimate loner, proposed that Speke be his sidekick.

It was a compromise, a surprise, and the greatest single indicator that Burton knew he could not complete his mis-

---

*A matriarchal Egyptian goddess worshipped as the patron of nature and magic.

sion alone. This was his last chance. Failure was not an option. Speke was not so much a fellow explorer as a safety net.

This sort of unconventional thinking, which involves not just the will to achieve a goal but a fixation on that positive outcome, is vital to all successful personal odysseys. It is not a coincidence that the eminent psychologist Charles Snyder titled his landmark 1991 study on hope *The Will and the Ways.*

Hope is not just the will to get someplace, but the process of finding the countless ways to get there. Snyder's hope theory supposes that the person who has hope also possesses the will and determination that goals will be achieved, and makes use of the complex set of different strategies at his or her disposal to see these dreams come true.

The difference between people like Burton, however, and those who don't make use of the brain's more freewheeling capabilities, is a vestige of our primitive selves that has been dubbed "the reptilian brain"—or, more colloquially, the lizard brain. This prehistoric portion of our brain is, quite literally, the sort of brain that a chicken or a lizard possesses. The lizard brain is devoted solely to staying alive and propagating the species—or, more specifically, to fear and pleasure. It's certainly not hard to imagine the carnal and adventurous Burton having an overdeveloped lizard brain. It might even be deemed his defining attribute.

The lizard brain is also in charge of reproduction of the species, which causes it to send out impulses designed to prevent failure—or death. A substance known as norepinephrine is released by nerve cells. This makes the heart pound faster, pupils dilate, throats tighten, and less blood flows to non-essential organs.

Left unchecked, the lizard brain floods the body with messages of anger and negativity. This creates an overwhelming sense of caution. At the lower end of the spectrum, the lizard brain is the result of procrastination. The lizard brain, for instance, causes writer's block, as an individual becomes overwhelmed by a project and becomes too fearful of failure to let the words pour forth. The lizard brain is the source of compromise, mediocrity, and lives not lived to the fullest. Because it is more focused on preventing failure than ensuring success, it allows for a long life, but not necessarily a bold or a happy one. This is the voice in our head that urges us to back off and go slow; to avoid the roller coaster and instead stroll the boardwalk.

The amygdala, the set of neurons governing the lizard brain, is activated by the body's stress response. So at the other end of the spectrum, it is that same jolt of adrenaline early man felt when staring down a lion on the African savanna. The lizard brain tried to save his life by urging him to run like hell.

But what if that primal man's family was starving, and that lion represented dinner? Or its great tawny hide represented warmth? Or maybe that rogue lion had been terrorizing his family, as the great lions of Tsavo* would do centuries

*The man-eaters of Tsavo were a pair of lions that ate 135 construction workers during the development of the Kenya–Uganda Railway in 1898. The 10-foot-long animals stalked the men like prey, sometimes even pulling them from their tents in the night. Both lions were shot and

later. Killing the lion would be necessary for their survival, and thus he would have to stand his ground and kill it.

Early man would do this by overriding the lizard brain. First he would take a slow deep breath to bring down his heart rate. Then he would face the reality that panic would not help him complete his task. Then he would allow his brain to be flooded with possible solutions. This might happen slowly at first, because the lizard brain would be screaming that killing a lion is impossible, because everything is impossible to the lizard brain. But if he remained calm and focused on completing his mission, those solutions would soon present him with possibilities.

All the while, the lizard brain would be screaming that he was about to die.

9

This is why the lizard brain is the enemy of hope. Dreams are sabotaged by its negativity. Thoughts of success are replaced by fear of embarrassment, shame, ridicule, and death— whether literal or emotional. In modern terms, this is the reason people don't pursue financially risky but emotionally stimulating careers, attempt public speaking (or public singing!), introduce themselves to the man or woman of their

---

killed after six months of terror. Their stuffed remains are on view at the Field Museum of Natural History in Chicago.

dreams, or attempt a marathon or any of a number of myriad other challenges that might make their lives richer and happier. Fear of public humiliation overwhelms them, and so they set their dreams aside as the lizard voice in their heads tells them they are too dumb, too ugly, too heavy, and most certainly doomed to failure—so why bother trying?

The lizard brain is why a curious and hopeful man such as Sir Roderick Murchison was more than happy to investigate and fund history's greatest explorations but unwilling to undertake even one of his own.

Curiosity and hope are also why that great Portuguese nobleman Henry the Navigator devoted his life to the sea. He built a great research and training facility that featured a library, nautical academy, astronomical observatory, and shipbuilding facility. Over time, he sponsored the design of a revolutionary new ship called the caravel. The caravel, with its triangular sail ("lateen" in nautical terms) and shallow draft (perfect for coastal sailing), allowed Portuguese explorers to navigate the treacherous reefs and shoals of the African coast. It was a design not too far removed from, but nevertheless an upgrade over, Brendan's hide-covered curragh. It was the caravel that allowed Bortolemeu Dias to round the Cape of Good Hope at the southern tip of Africa. This not only allowed Portuguese vessels to sail across the Indian Ocean to open the spice trade with Asia, it also meant they could sail north up the African coast and open a European market for Arab slave traders.

Columbus, most famously, sailed caravels on all four voyages to the New World.* The caravel was such a singular and unique vessel that it's safe to say that these journeys might never have occurred without its discovery.

Like Sir Roderick, however, Henry the Navigator never once sailed on an expedition. He had the resources, the power, and every other tool at his disposal to sail the world, but he never ventured outside Portugal.

Even among history's great explorers, there was a difference between those who learned to look at a problem from every angle, seeing hope where others merely saw "impossible," and those who were doomed midexpedition by the ongoing stress of a journey.

Consider the outcomes of two very different expeditions. In 1845, Sir John Franklin, an RGS founder and former governor of Tasmania, set out from England to find the Northwest Passage to Asia. In the same way that Columbus had hoped to sail west to the Orient through a southerly route, so Franklin was hoping to do the same by finding a route north of Canada. This would immeasurably enhance Britain's trade prospects. Taking into consideration all previously explored aspects of

---

*Columbus originally sought funding for his first expedition from the Portuguese. Dias's success in opening a new trade route to Asia put an end to that, causing him to seek funding from the Spanish instead. In an ironic twist, Columbus's ships were boarded off the Iberian coast after his first voyage of discovery, and Dias led the boarding party. Dias would drown on May 23, 1500, when his ship was lost in a storm.

this potential waterway, there were roughly 1,000 miles of the Canadian Arctic that needed discovering.

Franklin was fifty-nine at the time of his departure, and a veteran of three other Arctic expeditions. Despite his experience, the British Admiralty offered six other men the job before finally settling on him to lead this expedition. The two ships under his command were known as "bomb" vessels, based on the military armament of heavy mortars they carried in wartime. To withstand the vibration of firing these big guns, the hulls were designed for extra sturdiness, which made them perfect for polar exploration. Both HMS *Erebus* and *Terror** had already seen service in an 1840 expedition to the Antarctic.

Whatever concerns the Admiralty might have held about Franklin proved tragically correct. *Erebus* and *Terror* were soon lost in the Arctic, and to this day have not been found. It is known that they were trapped in winter ice and that Franklin and his men were forced to abandon the vessels and live on King William Island—named for the same William IV who established the RGS gold medal and provided its royal charter. It was an enormous landfall, the sixty-first biggest island in the world. It fell roughly halfway in the middle of the 1,000 uncharted miles Franklin needed to explore, and is home to im-

---

*Both ships would be immortalized in literary history. Joseph Conrad mentioned them by name in *Heart of Darkness* as a testimony to the perils of exploration. Jules Verne did the same in *20,000 Leagues Under the Sea*.

mense populations of caribou. Inuit Eskimo tribes have long inhabited the region.

It was September 1846 when Franklin's ships became hopelessly stuck. Clearly there was no longer an expedition at this point, because the trapped vessels would have been slowly crushed by the ice's incremental pressure. Both *Erebus* and *Terror* possessed ship's boats that could have been rigged with sails for a journey back through the relatively placid inland waters in summertime. Franklin chose not to do so, despite the rather obvious fact that no British sailor had ever sailed this way before, and thus rescue was highly unlikely unless it was self-initiated.

An entire winter and spring passed. This could not have been a pleasant waiting period. In addition to the crew's anxieties, King William Island is what is known as a polar semidesert. It is almost completely flat. Night lasts three or four months in winter. Day lasts just as long in summer. There are less than 6 inches of precipitation a year, the ground is perpetually frozen in a thick layer of permafrost, and the temperature doesn't rise above freezing for more than two months. More often, it remains more than 50 degrees below zero. There are few trees, but an abundance of moss and lichens. As sparse as the land can be, the sea is equally abundant, filled with walrus, narwhal, and beluga.

And polar bears.

The crews of both ships certainly would have seen these fierce predators as they sailed deeper into the Northwest Passage. Equally at home on land and sea, the polar bear has a bite force of 1,200 pounds per square inch (200 pounds more than a lion or a Bengal tiger, but only a third of saltwater crocodiles or hippopotamuses), can run 25 miles per hour, swim for hours in Arctic waters, and considers any living source of meat to be food—including man.

Whatever the reason, Franklin did nothing. By the time spring had turned to summer, he was dead. If it was his timid behavior that prevented his crew from seeking rescue, this might have been the perfect opportunity to do something bold. The men had spent nine months there, certainly long enough for someone to dream up a risky though ingenious plan to seek help. They also knew that the window of opportunity was small: the seas along King William Island are ice-free for only two months every summer. Time was of the essence.

And still they did nothing.

10

The men of *Terror* and *Erebus* waited another full year before attempting a walk back to civilization. There are no signs that they shot and ate caribou, or that they attempted to work with the Inuit to find a way out. Despite the severity of their circumstances and the cold, hard fact that no one was coming to rescue them,* the lizard brain in Franklin and his men

*An official search and rescue party wasn't launched until spring of 1848. Lady Franklin became a very public symbol of personal loss as it became clear that her husband and his men would never return.

chose to exercise caution and die miserably rather than con-
coct some daring plan to get back to civilization.

Every single man perished, whether from scurvy, tubercu-
losis, lead poisoning, or starvation. Worst of all, the crew grew
so desperate for food that the survivors began eating the dead
bodies of their shipmates. This meant that dying men knew
their bodies wouldn't be properly buried, but ravaged by their
friends. What an awful way to go to the grave.

This is what happens when the lizard brain takes control
of an expedition.

Seventy years later, another British polar expedition
would also see their ship crushed by winter ice, but with very
different results.

"Men wanted for hazardous journey," read the advertisement placed by Anglo-Irish explorer Ernest Shackleton, "small
wages, bitter cold, long months of complete darkness, constant
danger. Safe return doubtful. Honor and recognition in case of
success."*

There are many who doubt this famous advertisement actually existed, or that five thousand men and three women re-
sponded, as is so often stated. But the fact remains that when
Ernest Shackleton set off on his Imperial Trans-Antarctic

Ultimately, more than two dozen search parties were launched to find
Franklin. The graves of some crew have been found, but Franklin's body
is still missing.
*Many believe it was apocryphal. Real or not, it has only added to the
Shackleton legend.

Expedition in 1914, this veteran polar explorer was among the most famous men of his day. So great was his fame, and so enthralled were the British people by his expeditions, that he was given special permission to proceed with his voyage in August, despite the outbreak of what would be World War I just five days earlier. First Lord of the Admiralty Winston Churchill, who well understood the galvanizing manner in which great human achievement could rally a nation, personally gave Shackleton the final go-ahead.

Shackleton was a hard-drinking, charismatic man of the world. Bored by school in his youth, he shipped out as a sailor's apprentice at age sixteen and within eight years had risen to the rank of master mariner, qualified to command any British vessel on the high seas. But in 1901, at age twenty-seven, he sought a new form of adventure and secured a position with an expedition shipping out to explore the South Pole. The National Antarctic Expedition was the brainchild of RGS president Sir Clements Markham, a former naval officer who served on the 1851 search for the Franklin Expedition.* It would be the first British expedition to Antarctica since the 1839–43 voyage of Sir James Clark Ross, who charted great portions of its coast and named two great volcanoes after his

---

*Among other adventures. Markham is perhaps history's most diverse, prolific, and unknown explorer. He made extensive journeys into South America, Ethiopia, India, and the Arctic. Markham left the navy in 1851 to protest the use of corporal punishment on board ships, and was later responsible for allowing women membership into the RGS.

ships of exploration: Mount Erebus and Mount Terror—the same *Erebus* and *Terror* that Franklin would doom to polar ice five years later.

Markham's expedition would launch the careers of many famous explorers, among them Shackleton and Robert Falcon Scott, with whom Shackleton had a curt and acrimonious relationship. But although the journey would be a highly publicized success for all involved, it would be the making of Shackleton for a very different reason. He became gravely ill during a push south toward the pole with Scott and scientist Edward Wilson. All the men suffered from scurvy, frostbite, and snow blindness, but Shackleton was hit hardest. "Shackleton has been anything but up to the mark," wrote Wilson at one point, "and today he is decidedly worse, very short winded and coughing constantly, with more serious symptoms that need not be detailed here but which are of no small consequence one hundred and sixty miles from the ship."

Shackleton was sent home to convalesce. Scott made matters worse by writing critically about Shackleton's physical shortcomings in his book about the expedition. Shackleton considered his failure a disgrace, and pushed himself to ensure that such humiliation never happened to him again. However, his failures mounted. Back home in England, he suffered financial setbacks and ran unsuccessfully for political office. A second and successful Antarctic expedition from 1907 to 1909 made him a national hero. But even though his party went farther south than any previous expedition, they were

forced to turn around 112 miles from the pole, which had become his generation's version of finding the source of the Nile.
This Holy Grail of exploration would be reached by Swedish
explorer Roald Amundsen in December 1911. Amundsen
had also been the first man to traverse the Northwest Passage.
And with American explorer Robert Peary appearing to have
reached the North Pole in 1909,* there seemed to be nothing
for a great polar explorer like Shackleton to conquer.

So he devised something harder: a journey from one side
of Antarctica to the other. The Imperial Trans-Antarctic Expedition would be a logistical as well as a physical challenge
that would require one ship to drop his men off, and another
to wait for them on the far side. Resupply depots would be
set up at vital junctures along the coast. But while the expedition set sail to great fanfare, things soon went horribly wrong.
Endurance, Shackleton's vessel, became frozen in pack ice in
January 1915. After ten long months of drifting within the
ice, she began taking on water. Shackleton ordered *Endurance*
abandoned. She was crushed by ice and sank a month later.

By this time, Shackleton and his men were camped on an
ice floe. He hoped that the ice would drift toward the solid
ground of a small island. When this failed to occur, he shifted
his base to another ice floe. Finally, after six months of living
atop floating ice, Shackleton ordered his men into lifeboats,

---

*This is still in some dispute. Many believe Peary falsified his journals. If
so, Amundsen would lay claim to the triple crown of polar exploration
by making an undisputed journey to the North Pole in 1926.

and they paddled to the safety of a place called Elephant Island, nearly 400 miles from where *Endurance* rested at the bottom of the sea.

But they were still stuck. There is neither flora nor fauna on Elephant Island, a grim and mountainous place where winds can reach 100 miles per hour. The chances of a ship randomly sailing past and spotting them were almost non-existent. If Shackleton couldn't figure out a solution, he and his men would surely suffer the same fate as the Franklin Expedition.

History doesn't document Shackleton's thought process, so it is impossible to say how he found a solution to this impossible problem. Research into the life of Leonardo da Vinci, who was renowned for creative risk-taking, suggests that his process involved a series of seven questions: (1) *What* is the problem? (2) *When* does it need to be solved? (3) *Who* would benefit most from this problem being solved? (4) *How* can I motivate myself to solve this problem? (5) *Where* haven't I looked for answers? (6) *Why* is solving this problem important? And (7) *What if* this turned out to be the best thing that ever happened to me?

On the surface, those questions seem a bit lengthy. But imagine the breadth of da Vinci's creative genius, and realize that it would not take days or even hours to mull his decision. Imagine those questions being asked within a split second, as his brain went to work on a creative solution.

But that was da Vinci's method. Each of us has a different process. Maybe an individual leaves out a question or two. Maybe their brain works in such a way that it presents itself as an abstract concept or a theory. But we all indulge in creative problem solving. This is the link between da Vinci and Neil Armstrong; Thomas Edison and Lawrence of Arabia. Either way, the focus of the process is one clear and concise sentence bouncing around the inside of our cranium's interior walls again and again and again until a solution is found: get it done.

Get it done.

11

Shackleton came up with a bold and audacious plan. He would sail a small boat 800 nautical miles across the Southern Ocean* to South Georgia Island,† where whaling ships would help his men reach safety. Shackleton ordered his expedition's carpenters to transform the 22-foot lifeboat by strengthening the keel, raising the gunwales, and building a small covered deck out of wood and canvas, then making it watertight (almost) with paint and seal blood.

*A body of water contiguous to the Atlantic, Indian, and Pacific Oceans, beginning at 60 degrees south latitude. Its high salinity, pack ice, strong average winds (highest on Earth), and powerful Antarctic Circumpolar Current differentiate it from those other waters.
†Named by Captain Cook for George III, King of England at the time of his journey. George and his wife, Charlotte, were the recipients of more place names around the world than any two people in history, thanks to Cook's extensive travels.

In effect, Shackleton was using the acquired wisdom of the nautical age to transform an ordinary wooden lifeboat into a craft resembling a cross between a caravel and curragh—though smaller by almost half than Brendan's vessel. Despite the fact that it had been fifteen years since he left the seafaring world behind, he was subconsciously combing his mind for nuggets of wisdom that would help him succeed. Shackleton was preparing to brave monstrous seas and freezing hurricane-force winds on a journey through waters charted by Captain Cook. And he hoped—this is the most powerful word of all here, describing every breathtaking instant that would ensue—to combine all this knowledge to sail a distance greater than that from London to Africa. Shackleton was so sure of this hope that he refused to pack supplies for more than four weeks.

Not only did Shackleton succeed, but also upon arriving at South Georgia Island, he and three members of his five-man rescue mission were forced to march thirty-six hours over mountainous terrain to finally reach a whaling station. Imagine the countless number of times he needed to override the lizard brain. Problems ranged from calculating the trough of a wave to estimating compass headings to the preventing of hypothermia and frostbite. And throughout, Shackleton's leadership needed to be infused with hope. Without it, his men would consider their epic journey a suicide mission instead of something bold, attainable, and worth attempting.

Shackleton and all his men returned home safely to England, where he received a hero's welcome. But normal life bored him and he began drinking even more heavily. Six years later, at the age of just forty-seven, he died in bed of a heart attack.

At his widow's request, Shackleton's body was buried on South Georgia Island.

It lies there still.

12

The themes throughout Shackleton's exploration career would have been familiar to Burton and Speke: life-threatening adversity, rivalries within an expedition, the futility of being cut off without hope of rescue, and that overwhelming desire to find a way to succeed, if only to be spared public humiliation.

Indeed, bravery, rancor, and bitterness would become synonymous with their expedition after their journey into Africa. Burton had even begun to sow these seeds after the Somaliland debacle.

This is why his choice of Speke as a partner on the second African expedition was such a massive surprise.

Burton, in fact, was terrible to Speke after Somaliland. Burton spread rumors that Speke had been a coward during the attack on the beach, and that Speke retreated in the face of danger. As leader, Burton also had the right to confiscate the journals of all members of his expedition, a practice dating back to nautical exploration. Not only had he incorporated Speke's notes into his own book about the journey to Harar, but he also edited them in such a way that made Speke come across as an imbecile with no apparent command of putting together coherent sentences. One can only imagine Speke's embarrassment when *First Footsteps in East Africa* was published in late 1856.

It is likely that Speke's many strengths threatened Burton, and brought on these attacks. Certainly, Burton had no problem ignoring them when planning his new expedition. Speke possessed great physical endurance and a lack of fear. He was a risk-taker and adventure junkie, unsuited to the humdrum of daily British life. Speke was at home in the wilderness and able to navigate with great precision. He wasn't the sort of man to chatter on endlessly, which could become a source of irritation on a long journey. And finally, Speke needed the redemption as much as Burton. A successful journey would wipe away the smear of cowardice that now followed his name.

Most important of all, Burton recognized that Speke wouldn't quit. In reading all those published accounts about Africa while preparing his plan for the RGS, it had become clear to Burton that none of those previous explorers had much nerve. While writing boldly about their adventures in Africa, these authors hadn't gone very far inland from the coast. Yet Ujiji was 1,000 miles from the Indian Ocean. Burton required a man completely comfortable with leaving the safety of the coast behind.

Speke was such a man. He had been quite at ease traveling alone into Somaliland, hunting and exploring without fear while Burton made his way to Harar. He not only recovered from his savage stab wounds and temporary blindness, but also had downplayed the memory of their occurrence as he eagerly sought a return to Africa—perhaps to suffer more of the same. A quick study of Burton's good friends and other potential exploration partners revealed no other man with such courage.

Of course, Burton could have traveled into Africa alone. But truth be told, Burton's lizard brain still possessed a slight tug on his emotions. He would never admit as much, but the fiercely independent Burton was terrified of making the journey alone.

"It would scarcely be wise to stake success upon a single life," Burton explained to the RGS, explaining his need for a fellow explorer, "I should therefore propose as my companion, Captain Speke."

Burton's plan worked. In April 1856, he was granted the funding and permissions to explore the lakes region of central Africa.

There was just one other thing: he had yet to ask Speke.

Burton wasn't concerned in the slightest. Despite the bitterness and rancor and failure that threatened to bubble over and divide them, Burton knew that Speke possessed a powerful passion for Africa.

Speke, upon receiving the invitation by mail, accepted immediately.

The most recent European to attempt a similar journey into East Africa was a French naval officer. As bad as Burton and Speke suffered in Somaliland, this Lieutenant Mazan's fate was far worse. Warriors from the Mzungera tribe had taken him captive, tied him to a tree, and then ignored his screams and pleas for mercy as they cut off his bodily appendages one by one—with his head being the last to go.

Regardless of such dangers, Jack Speke and Dick Burton were on their way back into the land that nearly killed them, thrilled for the chance to once more risk their lives in the name of discovery.

"No phantom of the future cast a shadow upon our sunny path," Burton would write of the moment they began their adventure. "We set out, determined to do or die."

In the end, they would accomplish both.

PASSION

Of the gladdest moments in life, methinks, is the departure upon a distant journey into an unknown land.

—Richard Francis Burton, on the eve of
his journey into Africa with Speke

1

It was December 20, 1856, when Burton and Speke's sloop-of-war sailed into Zanzibar's Stone Town Harbor. The small island just off the African coast smelled sweetly of the clove plantations covering its rolling inland hills. The bone-white sands of the beaches and turquoise coastal waters mesmerized the two travelers, and the sense of enchantment was so strong that Burton described Zanzibar as "wrapped in a soft and sensuous repose, in the tranquil life of the Lotus Eaters, in the swoon-like slumbers of the Seven Sleepers, in the dreams of the Castle of Indolence."

Burton's overwriting aside, first appearances were deceiving. The shores along the main harbor were piled high with garbage, human waste, and even a floating corpse. Zanzibar had long been a crossroads of the Indian Ocean, a place where Arabs, Indians, Africans, Europeans, and even Americans came together to swap goods and services. The harbor was fronted by the consulates of various nations, with tall-masted ships poised to load and unload cargoes of spices, ivory, and people. The smell of cloves mingled with the equally powerful smell of the unwashed men, women, and children sweating freely in the tropical sun, soon to be sold at auction and packed tightly into the holds of those many resplendent vessels. Slavery did a booming business in Zanzibar. Those who died from floggings or illness were simply hurled into the sea, and those dead bodies washing ashore were quickly eaten by the packs of wild dogs roaming those pearly beaches. So while the island might have been more attractive to the eye than the coal piles of Aden, the home base for their first journey into Africa, in truth it was far more wretched.

Within two weeks Speke and Burton left the fetid confines of Zanzibar behind, with its epidemics of syphilis, "bad water and worse liquor," and then sailed across a narrow channel to the African continent to begin their journey.

Yet the expedition had arrived at perhaps the worst time of the year. The rainy season would soon be upon them, which would turn much of coastal Africa into muddy torrents and vast temporary lakes. So it wasn't until six months later, in

June of 1857, that Burton and Speke gathered on a beach just south of the small village of Bagomoyo to get under way. The newly hired caravan of porters was assembled, the red flag of the Zanzibar sultan was hoisted as a show of respect, and the Burton and Speke Expedition officially hit the trail. Their plan was to follow a well-trod slavers' path first navigated by the Arabs in 1825, stretching 745 miles from Bagomoyo to Ujiji, Burton's chosen destination.*

Bagomoyo would be the first of the "Three Jewels" to the Arab slave traders—stopovers where they might replenish themselves in safety and relative luxury while at work in Africa. The other two were Kazeh (now Tabora), in the heart of the savanna; and Ujiji, on the shores of the great shining lake named Tanganyika that no white man had ever seen.

Their guide was a short man with flat teeth named Sidi Mubarak Bombay, widely reputed to know all the great routes into the continent. Their caravan consisted of thirty-six porters and thirty pack animals laden with tents, hammocks, brandy, food, carpeting, compasses, sextants, cloth, beads, wire, daggers, swords, rifles, pistols, bullets, and cigars. The first miles away from the beach took them through a jungle morass of palm trees, strangler figs, and leopard orchids.

The mental image of a caravan is that of a long single-file line of African men carrying heavy loads on their shoulders,

---

*"The Central Slave and Ivory Trade Route," as it is now known, was submitted to the United Nations as a potential World Heritage Site by the United Republic of Tanzania in 2006.

followed by two white Englishmen carrying nothing at all. In fact, the truth was far more freewheeling. Concubines and camp followers trooped alongside the porters; protective guards from the Asian subcontinent known as *baluchis* provided an armed escort; and, instead of being completely African, the faces of so many in the convoy were half Arab or half Indian. This pointed to the obvious fact that while Africa was still a mystery to Europeans, Arabs and Indians had long ago made themselves at home.

An even closer look at the caravan would have revealed that Burton and Speke barely communicated. Despite having spent half a year together, basically doing nothing more than waiting for the weather to improve, the two were virtually unknown to one another. One would think that they had passed the time hanging out with the individual with whom they would soon tramp into the unknown—particularly since absolutely no one else would speak their language, and all they would have was each other.

Yet Speke, in Burton's words, was "a companion and not a friend, with whom I was strangers" that June afternoon. Speke preferred to march in front of the column, rifle in hand, while Burton rode a donkey at the rear. Speke was silent, where Burton was often fatuous. Speke was still miffed by Burton's high-handed behavior about the Somaliland failure, while Burton felt completely justified in his boorish attitude. Yet rather than air his frustrations, Speke chose to adopt the very Victorian attitude of keeping a stiff upper lip. He said nothing, but his anger ran quite deep. Speke would nurse his rage throughout their journey, eventually extracting his revenge in a most ingenious (and, to Burton's mind, deceitful) fashion.

Burton seemed oblivious to Speke's quiet loathing. He patronized Speke whenever possible, never missing the opportunity to paint him as an underling in his journals.

The daily ritual of caravan travel involved rising well before dawn, lighting the cooking fires in 3:00 a.m. darkness, and hitting the trail soon after. The oppressive African heat made this necessary, as it did numerous halts for rest when shade made itself available. Travel was sometimes just five or ten miles per day. In the early stages it was a trudge rather than an adventure, with Burton and Speke constantly on the watch for load bearers who planned to steal, desert, or even murder them. There was little attempt at friendship between the explorers and their employees, as this might be perceived as a sign of weakness. One day Burton, who had the advantage of being fluent in so many languages, overheard two men plotting to kill him. Without hesitating, he pulled his dagger, spun around, and stabbed one of them dead.

The other quickly fell to his knees and begged for mercy, which Burton granted.

2

The Victorian era of African exploration marked the first time since Homo sapiens stood upright and marched away from their forest hunting camps hundreds of thousands of years before, slowly crept into what would later be known as the Middle East and Europe, and then spread throughout the world, that his far-flung descendants were drawn back to the continent with the same sense of discovery that marked his exodus. But a breath in the greater scope of history, the heyday of African exploration was a seventy-year period that was both shorter than, and took place entirely within, the nineteenth-century reign of Britain's Queen Victoria.

Muslim traders from Arabia, Oman, and Persia had been doing business up and down the East African coast as early as 1200, but their interest revolved around monetary gain, not exploration. Thus their influence didn't extend inland at first. It was left to the Portuguese to send men into the interior, starting in the late fifteenth century. The heyday of African exploration, however, took place almost 250 years later. What a brilliant time to be an explorer, and what a perfect land through which to wander. For centuries, Africa had been so unwilling to give up her secrets that she was almost entirely uncharted. Cartographers were so mystified about what lay within the skull-shaped continent that they merely drew it black on maps and stamped the word "Unknown" (hence another reason for the "dark continent"*). Slowly, however, mythical cities such as Timbuktu were located and proven

---

*Weather, the unknown, and the dark skin tone of Africa's populace were all reasons for this term.

to be real, the sources of the Congo and the Zambezi were discovered, natural phenomena like Victoria Falls were seen by Europeans for the first time, and animals such as the gorilla became known to the outside world.

It was Paul Du Chaillu, later to become the inspiration for Edgar Rice Burroughs's *Tarzan*, who first reported that such creatures existed. Short, droopy-eyed, and given to speaking with a Cajun patois, the mixed-race explorer was always very mysterious about his origins. Sometimes he claimed to be from London, and other times Paris or New Orleans. In fact, he was born on that tiny volcanic island known as Réunion in 1831, the result of a dalliance between a French trader and his African mistress. Fifteen years later, when his father moved his business to the island of Cape Verde, on the opposite coast of Africa, Du Chaillu went along.

Through a whirlwind series of events, Du Chaillu made his way to America for his formal schooling, and then came back to Africa to begin his exploration career by collecting specimens for the Philadelphia Academy of Natural Sciences. After two successful journeys up the Ogobe River (he is credited with discovering gorillas and Pygmies), Du Chaillu retired to the Marlborough Hotel in New York to write children's books. A wanderer to the end, he died in St. Petersburg, Russia, in 1903.

Unlike nautical exploration, most men and women who traveled into Africa in the nineteenth century did not explore at the behest of a government. Their primary fuel was not duty, but passion.

Passion becomes an even more intriguing motivator when one realizes that the dangers awaiting Burton and Speke extended well beyond capture, torture, and bodily dismemberment.

Death seemed to be everywhere, from those corpses floating in Zanzibar's Stone Town Harbor to the very air that they breathed. Dysentery—that bloody, mucus-filled, endless torrent of diarrhea caused by parasitic, viral, and bacterial infections—was a very real threat, against which there seemed no defense. There was also the mysterious "fever," which broadly described any illness involving sweats, chills, and a drastically elevated body temperature. The heat and delirium came without warning or cause, striking virtually anyone, sometimes killing and sometimes not. There was no known cure.

This is how Congo explorer James Hingston Tuckey died in 1816. It could have actually been anything from cholera to typhoid fever that killed him. The Irish-born Tuckey spent eight months marching up the Congo, whose mouth is on the west side of Africa. The habit of purifying water through boiling was not yet common practice, so Tuckey's 300-mile upriver journey meant that he quenched his thirst each day by drinking water of many colors and textures, and absorbing countless unknown parasites and bacteria into his colon. Maybe it wasn't the water that caused Tuckey's high temperature and shakes, but something got to him. In the absence of modern forensics, or at the very least an autopsy, the vague "fever" was given as cause of death. As is so often the case with exploration, when news of

Tuckey's* demise reached England, a new wave of explorers were inspired to continue his unfinished work.

At least the disease known as malaria had a specific name. The air in Africa and other tropical climes could be very malodorous (Burton was revolted by the sight of people defecating openly on the beaches of Zanzibar, and the smells of raw sewage emanating from these otherwise idyllic white sands, which masked the otherwise intoxicating fragrance of nearby clove plantations), so medical officials were certain that the shaking, flu-like symptoms and anemia of malaria came through breathing bad air—hence, *"mal aria."* And while the idea that the air we breathe can cause illness seems antiquated or uninformed, the very real fact is that airborne pathogens in certain parts of Africa can cause severe sickness.

In 1880 it would be discovered† that malaria is caused by

---

*Tuckey is a tragic, forgotten figure who did a great deal to advance African exploration. He went to sea as a boy, and climbed through the ranks to receive his commission at the relatively advanced age of twenty-six. His ship was captured by the French in 1805, and he spent nine years as a prisoner of war. During that time Tuckey married fellow prisoner Margaret Stuart and whiled away the hours compiling the four-volume *Maritime Geography and Statistics*. His first assignment upon his release was the Congo expedition, which sought a way to connect the Congo with the rivers of inner Africa, a task that would be completed by Henry Morton Stanley eighty years later.

†Ronald Ross, a British officer in the Indian Medical Service, was the first to confirm that mosquitoes transmitted malaria. The theory was first put forth by French military doctor Alphonse Laveran nearly two decades earlier, for which Laveran was awarded the Nobel Prize in Medicine in 1907.

the bite of the female anopheles mosquito, which injects the disease into the human circulatory system, where it takes root in the liver and reproduces. But mosquitoes appeared to be nothing more than harmless annoyances to Burton and Speke. The African horse fly, on the other hand, had a bite that drew blood and was longer by a third than a honeybee. The African driver ant traveled in a swarm that ate everything in its path—including those human beings too old, infirm, or inebriated to get out of their path. Its bite is so powerful that African tribes often used the mandibles to suture open wounds. This was accomplished by allowing an ant to bite on either side of the gash. Once its jaws had locked into place, the rest of the body was snapped from the head, sealing the wound just as effectively as modern surgical staples.

A small innocuous brown fly known as "tsetse" seemed harmless, but was actually the cause of a deadly ailment known as sleeping sickness. Annually, this disease killed more people in Africa than lion, hippo, and crocodile attacks combined. Tsetse flies were such a scourge to horses and donkeys that explorers were reluctant to depend on them as pack animals, knowing that great swarms of flies would eventually infect them with their bites. This meant that local men were hired to carry these heavy loads on their shoulders. The Burton and Speke expedition would enlist more than a hundred such laborers.

And then, of course, death could come through those legendary and monstrous animals that haunted men's dreams. Of the world's dozen most dominant animal species,* six make their home in East Africa. The lion and crocodile (and even the wily hyena, with its bone-cracking jaws and ultrastrong stomach juices that allow digestion of these shards) were obvious perils. But perhaps most dangerous of all was the hippopotamus. Falling into one of the lakes or rivers that they called home could result in a brutal and violent death.

With their massive bulk, sharp tusks, and powerful bite force, these otherwise tranquil animals annually accounted for more human deaths than lions.

3

Speke was eager to add these specimens to his home museum, but a very real fact of life was that he would just as often be the hunted as the hunter. Days on the trail would mean long hours of marching, while nights would be spent inside a protective fencing of thorns known as a *boma* that his load bearers would build from scratch every day.

The boma would keep out the lions and hyenas, but not East Africa's extensive roster of killer serpents. The list reads like a who's who of venomous snakes: puff adder, Gabon

---

*A subjective list compiled by the author, defined as those land-based animals with total superiority and no physical rivals in their environment: cape buffalo, grizzly bear, polar bear, hippopotamus, salt water crocodile, rhinoceros, African lion, Bengal and Siberian tiger, bull elephant, and Nile crocodile.

viper, black and green mambas, boomslang, and several cobras—including the spitting cobra. There were also African rock pythons, which are not venomous, but can grow to twenty feet long, and are predatory enough to feast on juvenile Nile crocodiles.*†

While tracing the path of Burton and Speke across what is now Tanzania, I inadvertently saw each of these species up close and personal. The guesthouse where I was staying featured a long, dark hallway that linked its restaurant to the men's room. There was no light in this passage, but it was clear that the glass walls seemed to be moving as I made my way forward. Stopping to peer closer at this phenomenon, I instantly recoiled at the sight of a black mamba pressing its nose into the other side of the glass. I jumped straight backward and almost crashed into another glass case, this one filled with puff adders. In fact, inside each case lining the walls of this amateur herpetology collection were dozens of writhing, venomous snakes. The glass came from the thinnest of windowpanes—and was even cracked in several places, mak-

*Feral rock pythons have been discovered in the Florida Everglades since the 1990s, thanks to modern snake owners who dispose of their pets once they become too oversized to keep within the confines of a small home ophidiarium.
†Incredibly, the discovery of a new species of venomous viper was announced in 2012. Known as the Matilda viper, it has black and yellow scales, and devil's horns over its eyes. It is named for the daughter of the man who discovered it.

ing the display all the more terrifying. It's worth noting that a crocodile pen was at the far end of the hallway. And since the only way to or from the lavatory was through this eerie portal, I had to return to my dinner via the same path.

But at least glass stood between the snakes and myself. Passing through was as simple—and terrifying—as taking a deep, calming breath and walking very quickly.

There would be no such barrier protecting Burton and Speke on their daily march into the interior.

4

So there was tension as their journey began—between Burton and Speke, between the explorers and their caravan, between the various tribes and nationalities constituting the caravan, and between the entire party and ever-dangerous Africa. All the while, in the minds of Burton and Speke, was the memory of their failure in Somaliland, and the very real fact that they must not fail again.

In the midst of this palpable anxiety, a great tragedy occurred, one that might have stopped the expedition dead in its tracks if anyone had known about it. The fact that they didn't was perhaps the only bit of good luck Burton and Speke enjoyed in their journey's early days.

Here's what happened: their timepieces broke.

This might not seem like a big deal. The concept of time

would seem to have little bearing in a vast wilderness where schedules and social calendars have no place. So a little explanation is necessary.

Ironically, at the very same moment Burton and Speke were lumbering along the coastal plain, the Boston Watch Company in Massachusetts was launching the first-ever pocket watch made from standardized parts. By 1865 they would be turning out fifty thousand per year. These watches would prove vital to the expansion of America's railroad system, because proper timekeeping is important for avoiding collisions. This would have the added benefit of the railroads implementing intense standards to ensure that a watch not only worked, but was also easily readable and kept perfect time. Those railroad-grade pocket watches would later prove ideal for exploration, because precise measurements of time are vital to establishing east–west location—also known as longitude.* This, in turn, makes it possible to draw precise maps. And drawing precise maps is as vital to an explorer's job as the journey itself, allowing the global unveiling that takes place when a new location is revealed, and the words "Unknown" are replaced by the height of mountains and the courses of mighty rivers.

In June 1857, a timepiece portable enough to wear on

---

*The vertical lines on a map. Latitude are the horizontal lines, denoting the Earth's width. The shorthand "lat is fat" is a handy reminder when confused about which is which.

one's wrist* was still three quarters of a century away. The pocket watch standardization demanded by the railroads would not take place for more than forty years. Thus the Burton and Speke expedition were forced to carry three bulky marine chronometers to help measure longitude.

As it sounds, each timepiece was a precision instrument, designed for use on the high seas. The chronometers were housed in what appeared to be large mahogany music boxes. Each watch face was 4 inches across, and the box protecting it was 7 inches square. The clock casing was made of brass and the dials of steel. Each was spectacular to behold. One was even synchronized to the Royal Observatory back home in Greenwich, where the first accurate marine chronometer was invented by John Harrison in 1772.

Harrison's invention was among the most important in the history of exploration, because it added a bold new precision to cartography. It also changed the world in two other dramatic ways: First, it allowed Britain to co-opt time. For navigation purposes, ships at sea need a fixed time coordinate to determine their longitude. British authorities had already declared† that absolute noon would be the moment when the sun reached its highest point over Greenwich. The term "Greenwich Mean Time," to denote the universal day, was established on this calculation. The global breadth of the

*Wristwatches didn't come into vogue until the 1920s.
†In 1675, when the Royal Observatory was first built.

Victorian British Empire ensured that the rest of the world would soon base their local time on this moment. This is why we have time zones, so that each point on the map can designate noon similarly. Prior to this, localities and individuals depended upon solar time, as defined by sundials and the position of the stars, to schedule their days and seasons. The technology required to break time down into minutes and seconds was only available to the very wealthy, or to great observatories like that in Greenwich.

Second, the invention of the marine chronometer allowed Britain to designate itself as the home of longitude. Greenwich became the "prime meridian"—or, zero longitude—in 1851. Ships' captains throughout the British fleet understood these reasons perfectly well, because they always knew their precise distance from home. The rest of the world was left to wonder how a small suburb on the Thames had absconded with both time and travel.

Burton and Speke knew all this. They knew that they didn't just possess a random assemblage of marine chronometers, but timepieces with a pedigree linked to the home of time itself. The set was not just extraordinary, it was precious.

Yet these two intrepid explorers, men who knew that failure was not an option, allowed the chronometers to break.

And not just one of the timepieces—all three of them. Burton and Speke learned the hard way that a wooden box that works just fine perched atop the smooth surface of a ship's map table doesn't survive as well stuffed into a bundle worn across a porter's back for hours on end. This is particularly true when the porter is exhausted, and the bundle is hurled to the ground the instant the caravan comes to a rest.

Time seemed meaningless in those endless days marching through the coastal scrub defining the first 100 miles of Burton and Speke's journey. The 3:00 a.m. wakeups, the brutal marches, and, most of all, each man's first crippling bouts of malaria were much more immediate concerns. Their heads ached, their joints were stiff, they threw up, their skin turned yellow, they shivered uncontrollably, and their unseen though very swollen spleens gave them severe back pain, made it impossible to eat, and turned even the simplest cut or nick into an infection.

Small wonder that the chronometers went unused and unappreciated for three weeks; or that their careless destruction went undiscovered.

Without the ability to determine exact longitude, any maps drawn by Burton (though not Speke, as we will soon learn) would be imprecise and subject to questioning. Exact location would be impossible to pinpoint. Discoveries would be open to argument.

So why go on? Why continue a journey that has become pointless?

Because after three weeks, Burton and Speke had penetrated East Africa's coastal plain. The path had been uninteresting and there had been little in the way of discovery:

just small mud huts, termite mounds, and the pink backs of hippopotamuses rising above the brownish-green waters of the Kingani River like so many stepping-stones. Turning back would have rendered all that hard travel meaningless. The Africa they had come to see, with its reports of an endless savanna and snow-capped equatorial mountains, was almost within their reach.

In a word, the passion that had brought them to Africa was about to be realized.

5

Truly, passion was the only thing keeping them going. Anyone who has undertaken a lengthy expedition will testify that the things that matter most back home—in the case of Burton and Speke, fear of failure, need for redemption, approval of friends and family—become inconsequential in the wilderness. This is the reason why so many expeditions fail. Once those motivations are taken away, many find no reason to go on. The same can be said of almost any great objective.

Yet if there is a greater goal, and the perspective that even in the middle of nowhere, someone is keeping score of an individual's actions and behavior, the passion that enveloped the long journey at its inception does not fade.

Burton and Speke may not have liked each other, but they both possessed this fire. If possible, each possessed an overabundance. Most great expeditions have just one individual who owns the fervor to succeed at all costs. It is extremely rare to have two.

Far more common is the scenario where one man leads and a pack of naysayers engage in the daily task of tearing him down when times get tough. Yet despite their enormous social differences and worldviews, Jack Speke and Dick Burton shared an overwhelming passion for all things discovery. From the brilliance of the sunrise to the squabbling of their caravan, they were in the ironic position of being in their element while being completely out of their element—at the very same time.

Passion, in fact, is an emotion that seems tailor-made for Burton and Speke. It is ambition's fuel, leading us off onto the strange and sometimes unexpected tangents that define a life. And whether healthy (exercise, career, love) or destructive (compulsive exercise, workaholism, adultery), passion demands one very specific tribute: sacrifice. This act of giving up one thing (or everything) to completely pursue another is the definition of whether an activity is a passion or merely a fleeting fancy.

The word "passion" comes from the Latin verb *patoir*, which means "to suffer and endure." This is why the word attaches itself so easily to exploration, but is also used to describe the crucifixion of Christ—though it would not be until the twelfth century that someone made this connection. Interestingly, passion would not be used to describe sex, love, or enthusiasm for almost four hundred more years.

Passions are personal. They are obsessive, a source of joy, self-defining, and validating. The object of an individual's passion, so often irrelevant or irrational to others, is very often the burning ambition that gets them out of bed in the morning. This is because passion is derived from two seemingly contrary parts of the brain. The first is the caudate nucleus, the part of the brain that floods the body with the chemical dopamine when a positive result is achieved. Runners will know dopamine as the source of the "runner's high," and lovers everywhere will know it as the euphoria of a passionate new romance, when it feels impossible to keep their hands to themselves.

The second part of passion is more practical, derived from one of the brain's most advanced regions. The prefrontal cortex, as its name describes, is behind the forehead, right up at the front of the brain. This is where the tactics, planning, and calculations necessary to achieve a goal transpire. The prefrontal cortex is that logical part of the brain that tells a college student, for instance, to study first and attend a keg party afterward—rather than the other way around. The next time you find yourself focused on a plan or a scheme, and wonder why it seems like there is a lot of commotion in the front of your skull, it's because the cells of the prefrontal cortex are busy at work.

Thus every hard-fought success—thanks to the prefrontal cortex—is rewarded by immense personal and emotional well-being, courtesy of dopamine. Work and reward. Work and reward. Passion is our inner Pavlovian process. It's no wonder that we become consumed by our desires.

Passion is where we step out of our comfort zones. Each journey of exploration–global or personal—starts with curiosity and builds to hope, but passion is where it kicks into gear. It is the poetry that bursts forth from the previously stifled; the daily dedication to fitness from the newly healthy; and that decision to not delay life's greatest adventures until retirement age, but to live each and every day from this moment forward to its fullest.

6

I would consider the case of John Harrison and his lifetime obsession with building marine chronometers to be a powerful example of passion. But Ewart Grogan goes him one better—much better. The fourteenth of twenty-one children born to the surveyor general to Queen Victoria, and named after British prime minister William Ewart Gladstone—who also happened to be his godfather—Grogan developed a fondness for mountaineering in his teen years. During a family vacation to Switzerland following his father's death he immersed himself in climbing the local peaks, hoping to gain acceptance into the legendary Alpine Club, the world's oldest mountaineering association. It took him four years, but at age nineteen, Grogan realized his goal of being elected to the Alpine Club—whereupon he quit climbing and entered Cambridge to study law.

But the adventurous spirit that led the six-foot-tall Grogan to climb mountains was not quite done with him. In short order he was expelled for a number of pranks and run-ins with the law, volunteered to join the army and wage war in southern Africa against a Zulu uprising, and subsequently became so ill with blackwater fever, amoebic dysentery, malaria, and an abscessed liver that he was initially given up for dead and almost buried alive. Even after Grogan finally recovered, he still found a way to hasten his demise: Ewart Grogan fell in love.

Her name was Gertrude Watt, and she was the shy oldest sister of a Cambridge friend. The family estate was on the North Island of New Zealand, and it was at the invitation of Eddie Watt that Grogan had sailed there to recuperate from the African illnesses still coursing through his body.

Gertrude soon grew equally fond of the quick-witted Grogan. Yet when he asked her stepfather for her hand in marriage, Grogan was quickly shot down. Gertrude's father had invented the steam engine, and she was heir to a considerable fortune. Grogan, on the other hand, had no prospects and no income. He was, in the words of stepfather James Coleman, "drifting down the river of life without a rudder."

The year was 1897. The scene was played out in a large drawing room, in a villa containing forty rooms. The palatial home faced east, toward Hawke's Bay, first charted by James Cook in 1769, who also named it after Sir Edward Hawke, the first lord of the Admiralty who had launched Cook's exploration career. The Pacific stretches ever eastward from Hawke's Bay, not encountering a single landfall at the same thirty-nine degrees south latitude until the coast of Chile, almost 8,000 storm-tossed miles away.

So that particular drawing room was an evocative location, and it would not be too great a leap to believe that the stunning view from its windows conjured up thoughts of adventure and global travel. But it was the view of blue-eyed Gertrude that enchanted Grogan more than anything. And so, as he looked out over literally a sea of possibility, the twenty-two-year-old Grogan suggested a rather astonishing wager to prove his worthiness: he would walk from Cape Town to Cairo—the southern tip to the northern tip of Africa. It was a distance of almost 5,000 miles, and one that no man in history had ever accomplished.

"I can only assume you are trying to be funny," Coleman replied coolly.

"I am quite serious," replied Grogan. "Never more so."

There was no way Grogan could back down. An overwhelming sense of passion had led him to venture into the audacious, and he was now quite stuck with whatever happened next.

Coleman was incredulous. "My good man, do you realize what that would mean?"

"Perfectly."

The journey lasted two and a half years. In February of 1900, Ewart Grogan arrived in Cairo.

On April 30 of that year, he became the youngest man ever to address the Royal Geographical Society—of which he was later named a Fellow. He subsequently met separately with Queen Victoria and Henry Morton Stanley to speak of his journey.

And on October 11, 1900, Ewart Grogan and Gertrude Watt wed at Christ's Church in London, before a crowd of hundreds. They remained married until Gertrude's death almost forty-three years later.

7

So it was with the explorers. They didn't just set out on journeys; they undertook them with a powerful passion. They researched the lands through which they would travel, read the journals of explorers who had gone ahead of them, then lived each day as if it were their last. Ann Davison, the first woman to sail single-handedly across the Atlantic,* described exploration as "one of those rare glorious experiences that lift you out of the commonplace on to Olympian heights of delight," as if each journey fulfilled some deeper part of her being.

Passion can be seen most clearly—even today—all due to a monumental discovery that took place in India in the year 1852, in the town of Dehra Run, some 100 miles north of Delhi. Sir Andrew Waugh was sitting in his office at what was known as the Grand Trigonometrical Survey. He had spent the

*Something about turning forty left a mark on many an explorer. Perhaps it's just coincidence, but Davison, Cook, and Columbus all set out on their journeys at this point in their lives.

last thirty years of his life mapping the Indian subcontinent. Working from south to north, the survey had come within sight of the Himalayas in 1830, but the peaks were so massive and the valleys so deep that measuring them with normal instruments was prohibitive.

It wasn't until 1847, after the rest of India had been entirely mapped, that Waugh and his surveyors reluctantly focused their attention on charting the Himalayas. Their efforts were hampered each October to December by monsoons, and the peaks were so massive that the surveyors could only make accurate readings by placing their tools more than 100 miles away. Yet by August of that year, Waugh's team had succeeded in measuring a peak that the locals called Kangchenjunga. After taking readings from three different angles, the Grand Trigonometrical Survey certified that it was 28,156 feet high, making it the tallest mountain in the world.

The news would have been cause for celebration were it not for one thing: when Waugh went out in the field to observe Kangchenjunga, he noticed a second peak directly behind it that appeared to be slightly taller. Waugh named this "Peak B" and ordered his surveyors to march into the mountains to make more accurate measurements. Five long years later, Radhanath Sikdhar, the head of the survey's computing office, rushed into Waugh's office without knocking. "Sir," Sikdhar announced. He wore a high white turban and a bushy black beard. "I have discovered the highest mountain in the world!"

But what to do about it? This summit that Waugh soon renamed Peak XV (then renamed it for Sir George Everest, the surveyor-general of India from 1830 to 1843 and vice president of the Royal Geographical Society from 1862 until his death in 1863) was so remote that even finding a path to its base was problematic. Navigating the nips and tucks of its many valleys and ridges to find a route to the top would be a monumental feat of exploration in and of itself.

So for seventy-five long years Everest just sat there, as it had since the beginning of the world. The mountain represented Earth's last great exploration challenge. The poles had been reached and the great rivers charted when, finally, in 1921, seventy-four years after Sikdhar's pronouncement to Waugh, the British turned their attention to Everest.

Mountaineering wasn't invented on Mount Everest (Alexander the Great's troops climbed the Sogdian Rock in what is now Afghanistan way back in 327 BC). It only seems that way. Mankind's efforts to climb the world's seven highest peaks marked a new age in exploration, that of vertical discovery. From Mount Kilimanjaro* in Africa to Mount McKinley† in North America, the race to summit the world's tallest mountains became a fixation.

The climbing community was small, a band of like-minded men and women who reveled in doing something

---

*First summited in 1889 by German climber Hans Meyer and Austrian Ludwig Purtscheller.
†In 1913, by Alaska native Walter Harper.

previously impossible by defying gravity as they clambered straight up sheer rock faces. Climbers not only invented a new form of exploration, but out of necessity, also designed the new forms of equipment such as carabiners, dynamic rope, climbing harnesses, and even tents that allowed them to sleep overnight while dangling thousands of feet above a valley floor. Traditional duties of exploration such as cartography and anthropology were unnecessary and ignored. Their bodies learned to cope with the rarefied air of high elevations, including a "death zone" above 26,000 feet.* A condition known as hypoxemia kicks in at such great altitude, depriving the blood of oxygen. The effects can be gruesome: retinal hemorrhaging, fluid in the lungs, the sort of unsteady walk seen most often in drunks, nausea, severe headaches, and a fatal swelling of the brain.

No previous band of explorers had ever dealt with such a reality. The use of supplemental oxygen cylinders—in essence, the practice of bringing along their own air—would one day benefit aviation, underwater exploration, and lead to the development of pressurized airplane cabins. It can be said that without mountaineering, modern air travel would not exist.

Mountain climbing was defined by its panoramic views, feats of balance, legendary bouts of endurance, self-sufficiency, constant threat of sudden death, ability to remain completely

---

*A term first coined in the 1952 book *The Mountain World* by Swiss doctor Edouard Wyss-Dunant.

in the moment, and the all-too-crucial requirement that getting back to the bottom was as important as getting to the top. "Climb if you will, but remember that courage and strength are naught without prudence, and that a momentary negligence may destroy the happiness of a lifetime. Do nothing in haste, look well to each step, and from the beginning think what may be the end," wrote Edward Whymper, the Briton who became the first man to ascend the Matterhorn, in 1865.

Modern readers can also thank mountaineers for another profound, but often unnoted, contribution to exploration. The traditional means of describing an expedition were functional, and even boring, taking their cue from the dry notations in a ship's log. Later generations of explorers went completely in the opposite direction, overwriting to such an extent that their journals are either detailed research tools or Victorian sleeping pills. I have absolutely no idea how the British public thrilled to the writings of Burton, Speke, and the other great adventurers of the day. Both men write as if they had to validate each and every step of the journey, describing each situation and confrontation in exhaustive detail. Good for guys like me, trying to get inside their heads as I write a book. Not so good for that person hoping for a ripping read on an eight-hour train ride.

Enter the mountaineers. There were no indigenous people or their habits on which to opine at 25,000 feet. No tidal charts or shoal depths to be measured. Just some of the most stunning and dangerous beauty the world has ever known.

Mountaineers were so thoroughly impassioned by what they felt and saw as they climbed, that the words they put on the page were rhapsodic, imbued with a hyperbolic poetry long missing from written accounts of earlier explorations.

"On this proud and beautiful mountain we have lived hours of fraternal, warm and exalting nobility. Here for a few days we have ceased to be slaves and have really been men. It is hard to return to servitude," wrote Lionel Terray, a French climber who not only made a number of first ascents (the climbing term for being the first person in history to stand atop of a peak), but also put his climbing skills to functional use while battling Nazi Germany's mountain troops during World War II.*

Terray, who clearly used the mountains as a tonic for the worries of the modern world, would also go on to write that "If the conquest of a great peak brings moments of exultation and bliss, which in the monotonous, materialistic existence of modern times nothing else can approach, it also presents great dangers. It is not the goal of *grand alpinisme* to face peril, but it is one of the tests one must undergo to deserve the joy of rising for an instant above the state of crawling grubs."

Maurice Herzog, who along with fellow Frenchman Louis Lachenal became the first men to summit Nepal's 26,545-foot Annapurna in 1950, wrote beautifully about the strange ad-

*Climbers, desert explorers, and nautical adventurers have all used their expertise in wartime.

diction of shared misery. "Together we knew toil, joy and pain. My fervent wish is that the nine of us who were united in the face of death should remain fraternally united through life.

When individuals are forced to work together for long periods, in difficult scenarios, their best—as well as their worst—qualities come shining through. "The team," as French explorer Pierre Chevalier wrote, "must work together as one man and must consist of the best human material."

In the case of most of the mountaineers, the intensity of this *in extremis* bond often lasted only as long as the climb. Afterward came the letdown, and the inevitable search for a new adventure that would match the thrill of the climb. The Annapurna expedition, for instance, was a who's who of French climbers—Lachenal, Gaston Rebuffat, the indomitable Terray—and Herzog, a Parisian businessman who hired these montagnards* to lead him to the top. Though only two of them reached the summit, all four got very close—so close, in fact, that they were forced to spend the night in a single sleeping bag to avoid dying on the descent. Frostbite later resulted in the emergency amputation of all of Rebuffat's toes. For good measure, the threat of gangrene meant that Herzog had to have his fingers cut off, too. Yet the four men returned to France as heroes. That should have been enough glory for four alpine purists, but Herzog chose to shine the spotlight only on himself by publishing a heroic account clearly biased

*French, meaning "people from the mountains."

in his favor. *Annapurna* sold eleven million copies and made a legend of Herzog, allowing him to forsake the mountains for politics. Among other honors, he was awarded France's Legion of Honor, the nation's highest award. He later became a member of the International Olympic Committee.

But Rebuffat kept climbing. He put up forty new climbing routes in the Alps and advanced the now widely accepted notion that a climber was not conquering a peak, but working in communion with its grandeur.

The other two died in mountain accidents, with Terray falling from a cliff face at age forty-four and Lachenal plunging into a crevasse while skiing. He was just thirty-four, and five years removed from Annapurna. Appropriately, both men died in Chamonix, the spiritual home of French mountaineering.

When Lachenal's journals were on the verge of being published posthumously, Herzog took possession and scrubbed out all references that made himself look anything less than heroic. It was only much later that the actual diaries were discovered. Herzog, it should be noted, did not share his formidable royalties from *Annapurna* with the men who made it possible.

So it is that life intrudes on even the idyllic splendor of mountaineering, just as it ultimately imposes itself on all successful explorers. Returning home has always bedeviled the adventurous. The routine and status quo of daily life proved baffling after days and weeks and years of tripping the light fantastic. This was the explorer's curse.

8

The defining climbing quotation came from Everest's original and foremost explorer, George Mallory: "The first question which you will ask and which I must try to answer is this, 'What is the use of climbing Mount Everest?' and my answer must at once be, 'It is of no use.' There is not the slightest prospect of any gain whatsoever. Oh, we may learn a little about the behavior of the human body at high altitudes, and possibly medical men may turn our observation to some account for the purposes of aviation. But otherwise nothing will come of it. We shall not bring back a single bit of gold or silver, not a gem, nor any coal or iron. We shall not find a single foot of earth that can be planted with crops to raise food. It's no use. So, if you cannot understand that there is something in man which responds to the challenge of this mountain and goes out to meet it, that the struggle is the struggle of life itself upward and forever upward, then you won't see why we go. What we get from this adventure is just sheer joy. And joy is, after all, the end of life. We do not live to eat and make money. We eat and make money to be able to enjoy life. That is what life means and what life is for."

Or as Mallory later condensed his answer into a more succinct sound bite for a *New York Times* reporter: "Because it's there."

Between 1921 and 1953, some fifteen expeditions attempted to climb Everest. All but four were British. Twelve

people died in that time, with cause of death ranging from ava-
lanche, to pneumonia, brain hemorrhage, exhaustion, falling ice,
freezing, and perhaps most chilling of all: disappearance. This
was the fate of Mallory, who perished high on Everest in 1924
and whose body went undiscovered for seventy-five years. The
bitter cold had preserved his remains, which were buried under
a cairn by his discoverers. An Anglican service was held to con-
secrate the moment. It's worth noting that at 26,760 feet, Mallory's is the highest formal burial spot on Earth.

No one would reach the summit of Everest until 1953,
when a young man with a passion for mountaineering finally
set foot on the roof of the world. His name was Edmund Hillary, and he was sixteen when he first gazed upon Mount Rua-
peho on New Zealand's North Island during a school field trip.
He was immediately smitten by the desire to climb it. Though
that marked the first time in his life that the beekeeper's son
had seen a mountain covered in snow, it wouldn't be the last.

Eight years later, while serving as a conscientious objec-
tor to New Zealand's participation in World War II (he was
eventually drafted anyway), Hillary undertook a meditative
journey to New Zealand's Southern Alps, hoping to discern
a career path. He came to the unlikely conclusion that he
should dedicate his life to mountaineering. "I retreated to a
corner of the lounge filled with a sense of futility at the dull,
mundane nature of my existence," he wrote of a morning at
the base of Mount Cook. Out of the corner of his eye, he
watched as two climbers strode into the lounge, fresh from

reaching the summit. "Those chaps, now, were really getting a bit of excitement out of life. I decided then and there to take up mountaineering. Tomorrow I'd climb something!"

That passion drove Hillary for the next thirty years of his life. Though seriously injured in a plane crash in the South Pacific during the war, Hillary went ahead with his ambition once the conflict ended. He was pleased to discover that he was a natural mountaineer. By 1951 Hillary had climbed all over the world, and visited the Himalayas for the first time as part of an all-New Zealander expedition to Nepal. Within three years he was participating in a British-led expedition to climb Everest.

The original leader of the expedition was famed mountaineer Eric Shipton,* but he was replaced at the last minute by John Hunt, a veteran climber and World War II veteran who was said to have been a distant relation to Dick Burton. Hillary was chosen as one of Hunt's two teams that would attempt the summit. When the first two-man group turned back due to exhaustion, Hillary and Sherpa guide Tenzing Norgay belatedly got the nod. On the morning of May 29, 1953, they set out from their tents at 6:30 a.m. Hillary fell at one point and suggested turning back, but without further discussion they went on. The pair reached the South Peak by 9:00 a.m., and then followed the saddle leading to the very top. By 11:30 they were on the summit. Hillary was first, followed by Tenzing. They stayed on the peak for a half hour. Hillary snapped a pic-

*Winner of the RGS Patron's Medal in 1938.

ture of Tenzing, but the Sherpa didn't know how to use a camera, so there is no picture of Hillary on the roof of the world.

The news of their accomplishment reached London on June 2, 1953,* the very day that Elizabeth was crowned queen. As one of her first official acts, she knighted Hillary.

Exploration haunted those who pursued its calling. Passion is the reason. The proof isn't in the journey, but in what happened afterward. Once an explorer returned home and the public acclaim died down, what followed were almost inevitable thoughts of getting back out there so they could do it again, do it better, and travel farther into the unknown. A single expedition would have been a life-changing experience to a normal wanderer, but an overwhelming majority of history's most successful explorers were not satisfied with just one. They wanted more. And more. Until in many cases it not only cost them their lives, but also consigned their corpses to mutilation and anonymity. Which is why great passion also requires great discretion if it is to be properly harnessed. The lack of this key attribute was the downfall of many a great explorer.

Edmund Hillary narrowly avoided this fate. He returned to the Himalayas in 1954, only to lose an expedition member in a deep crevasse and break three ribs trying to save the man's life. The following year he crossed Antarctica from one side to the other by a motor-powered Sno-Cat, becoming the

---

*The reporter breaking the news was legendary journalist and travel writer James—now Jan—Morris. For my money, she's one of the great writers of our time.

first man in history to do so. In 1960, Hillary returned to the Himalayas once again, this time on an unsuccessful hunt for the abominable snowman.* It was only after his wife and teen-age daughter were killed in a plane crash in 1975 that Hillary retired to his bee farm outside Auckland.

9

The great polar explorer Roald Amundsen, however, was not so lucky. In the course of his career, he traveled to the South Pole and the North Pole. He was definitely the first man to reach the former, and there's evidence he may have also been first to the latter. Amundsen designed and sailed the small ship *Maud* through the Northwest Passage (over North America) and attempted the Northeast Passage (over Siberia), neither of which had been accomplished before. He endured polar winters and polar bear attacks. One time, he deliberately allowed the *Maud* to become frozen in pack ice so that she might simply float with the currents. Amundsen was an explorer his entire adult life. He knew nothing else. So even when he'd conquered the poles he kept coming back for more, as he did in 1928, when he went looking for Italian explorer Umberto Nobile, whose dirigible had crashed while flying over the North Pole. Nobile was subsequently rescued, but Amundsen

---

*Which is not as farfetched as it seems. Shipton had taken a photograph of a purported abominable snowman print in 1947. Clearly etched in the snow, the footprint was longer than the climber's ice ax.

was not the man who located him. Amundsen's body is still out there,* despite years of intense search efforts. The most likely reasons for his disappearance were either death by drowning or an attack by polar bears, who dine on both fresh kills and carrion.

Captain James Cook also suffered from lack of discretion. He retired after his second voyage of discovery and was rewarded with a well-paying and prestigious job onshore, only to grow despondent for the explorer's life within weeks. He begged to return to the sea for what would become his ill-fated third voyage. As we've already seen, his body suffered the indignity of being cooked and eaten.

The great African explorer David Livingstone, who should have been veteran enough to be the standard-bearer for discretion, also fell prey to the siren's song of exploration. Like Amundsen and Cook, he too embarked on one last ill-fated voyage. To read Livingstone's words as he set out on that final journey is to assume that his life was carefree. In fact, he was burdened by failure. Livingstone screwed up more often than he succeeded. He was once almost eaten by a lion. His eldest son felt so abandoned by his perpetually absent father that he snuck off to America, enlisted in the Union Army, and died in the Civil War. Livingstone's wife became an alcoholic and

*Like many explorers, Amundsen had frequent money problems. His beloved *Maud* was sold to pay his creditors. She later sank in Cambridge Bay, Canada, where her hull can still be seen protruding above the shallow waters.

threw herself at men—bad form for anyone, particularly the wife and daughter of missionaries. When Mary Livingstone summoned the courage to join her husband on a trip up the Zambezi River, she promptly made a cowardly nuisance of herself before dying of malaria. On that same expedition during the years 1858–64 (Livingstone would return home just in time to referee the Nile Debate) the group's physician declared that Livingstone was "Out of his mind and an unsafe leader."

This lunatic of whom the good doctor is speaking is the same David Livingstone who was considered the greatest, most beloved, and most famous explorer of his day. Livingstone's worldwide fame was so great that one poll showed only Queen Victoria to be more popular.

Livingstone is an example that failure is not fatal. It is just as much a natural by-product of passion as success. Great explorers such as Livingstone used failure as a valuable learning tool that would assist them on their next journey. Lesser explorers, most of whose names have long been forgotten by history, simply gave up.

Even in the midst of that deeply flawed Zambezi journey, Livingstone vowed to never quit exploring. "I will go anywhere," he wrote, "provided it is forward."

These words would prove prophetic. He returned from the Zambezi in 1864 and was back in Africa to start yet another journey by 1866. It began well enough. "The mere animal pleasure of traveling in a wild unexplored country is very great," he wrote after setting out into what is now Mozambique. "The body is soon well knit; the muscles of the limbs grow hard and seem to have no fat. The countenance is bronzed and there is no dyspepsia."

Whereupon Livingstone got famously lost—and stayed that way for six years. His fame ensured that people around the world began wondering about what had happened to him. In England, Sir Roderick Murchison wrote constantly to the *Times* of London, reassuring readers that rumors of Livingstone being eaten by cannibals or killed by hostile tribes were all nonsense. Murchison did everything in his power to support Livingstone—except, of course, send a search party.

Much to Murchison's chagrin, the American newspaper the *New York Morning Herald* launched a covert Livingstone rescue operation. Reporter Henry Morton Stanley marched alone into Africa and found him in Ujiji, of all places.* Stanley not only located the now-destitute Livingstone, but also provided him with a fresh batch of supplies. This allowed Livingstone to continue his explorations even though he was nearly

---

*There is discrepancy over whether Stanley's famous "Dr. Livingstone, I presume?" line was ever actually spoken. A glance at Stanley's journals shows that portion of the page ripped from the book, so the truth will never be known. The words were meant to make him sound genteel, but in time they would become a vaudeville punch line that Stanley abhorred.

sixty years old, had almost no teeth, and had reached a point in his travels where it was quite clear that he had no intention of ever returning to civilization.

Stanley left Africa to tell the world he had found Livingstone, becoming forever famous in the process. His original greeting to the lost explorer—"Dr. Livingstone, I presume?"—would become the best-known quotation in the annals of exploration. Stanley was proud of the comment when he first slid it into a dispatch to the *Morning Herald*, even though ample evidence points to the fact that he never actually said those words. But it would haunt him for the rest of his life. Stanley would come to regret that he ever claimed to have uttered those words, which remain his greatest legacy to this day.

Meanwhile, Livingstone chose to remain behind on his beloved continent, continuing his daily process of "bashing on, regardless," as he liked to say. Livingstone not only disagreed with Burton and Speke's theories about the source of the Nile, but also thought its discovery beneath his considerable talents. He had intentionally ignored it for the first twenty-five years of his career. However, he also considered Africa his sole domain. It riled him when Burton and Speke became famous. If anyone was going to find the source, he was determined that it would be him, if only to reclaim the mantle of top African explorer.

Sadly, Livingstone's theories were wrong. He was 1,000 miles south of the source by April 1874—and marching in the opposite direction. There was no way he would ever find it. Burton and Speke—or one of them, at least—was right about its location.

By then, Livingstone was literally walking in circles around East Africa. One night, the former missionary got down on his knees to pray at bedtime, only to topple forward onto his pillow as his body finally gave out. Cause of death could have been any of a number of the maladies coursing through his system, courtesy of African exploration: anemia, malaria, and/or the rampant course of violent dysentery that had been forcing him for weeks to step off the trail and relieve himself every few hundred yards. It's worth noting that "fever" was never considered. The man whose physical health was once so robust that he bragged of drinking water "putrid with rhinoceros urine and buffalo dung" had become a living petri dish. The surprise is not that he died from all those bugs and bacteria, but that they took thirty-three years of exploration to do him in.

The body was discovered the next morning. Livingstone's loyal assistants, knowing precisely what they must do next, made an incision into Livingstone's lower abdomen and removed his internal organs. The heart was buried under a baobab tree, so that a part of the explorer might always remain in his beloved Africa. Livingstone's corpse was then mummified by stuffing it with salt and sand, and then drying it in the sun for two weeks. Chuma and Susi, as these assistants were named, then wrapped Livingstone in bark and sailcloth and hand-carried him more than 1,000 miles back to the coast.

The body was placed on a British ship and returned to England, where he was buried in the nave of Westminster Abbey.*

10

Passion made Livingstone successful, made him famous, made him fearless, cost him his family, gave him a small fortune,† heightened his ambition, killed him, and led to his heroic burial. Nothing great in this world happens without passion, but it is also a dangerous thing, and not to be taken lightly. It is the TNT of our emotional makeup: fragile to manage, capable of great destruction, and the instrument for stunning achievement.

Nowhere is this more obvious than the breakthrough moment in which Speke saved the collective behinds of himself, Burton, and the entire expedition. The man whom Burton so often tried to paint as mentally inferior ingeniously invented a method for gauging longitude without the broken marine

---

*Henry Morton Stanley was one of his pallbearers. Stepping out of the church, Stanley vowed to continue Livingstone's work. This ultimately led to Stanley marching from one side of Africa to the other, in what is easily the greatest expedition in history. Stanley not only completed Livingstone's work, but also that of the ill-fated Congo explorer James Hingston Tuckey from 1816. Stanley named an enormous rapids on the Congo River the Livingstone Falls, for his mentor. Nothing was named for Tuckey.

†Livingstone was penniless as his final journey got under way. The post-mortem sales of his journals provided quite handsomely for his heirs.

chronometers. Using a sextant, a *Nautical Almanac,* and a four-ounce rifle ball attached to a string, Speke was able to figure Greenwich Mean Time by shooting the moon and recording its angle to various stars. Night after night after night, Speke peered into the nighttime sky and honed this new skill. His ingenuity was extraordinary, particularly in light of the fact that Burton did absolutely nothing to help, and showed no interest in finding a new method of determining longitude. In time, Speke's lunar distances proved to be so accurate that even the jaded Burton was awed—though he tried very hard to appear unimpressed.

Needless to say, the expedition was resuscitated. And though both men were once again grappling with malaria's delirium and shakes as August turned to September, they could both rejoice in the knowledge that the coastal plain was behind. At long last, the African savanna lay before them. On November 7, 1857, exactly five months after setting out, Burton and Speke arrived in the Arab trading post at Kazeh.* They had traveled 600 miles in 134 days. They were eagerly adopted by the Arab sultans, who housed them in a small cottage and lavished them with beef, coffee, cakes, and other vestiges of civilization.

But even in this moment of great accomplishment, there was conflict between Burton and Speke. The schism between

---

*Now known as Tabora, and most easily accessed by plane or by the railway running from one side of Tanzania to the other, hewing closely to the same Arab slave path followed by Burton and Speke.

them had never healed during their many months of travel, and Burton soon widened it by using his fluent Arabic to glean new nuggets of geographical information from their hosts—none of which he shared with Speke. The gist was this: a powerful river flowed out of a large lake a few hundred miles north of Kazeh. A second lake, 200 miles due west, also existed. This was the lake on which their original destination of Ujiji was located.

Unfortunately for Burton, Speke figured out that something funny was going on. He used his knowledge of Hindustani to learn what the Arabs had been sharing with Burton, and then enthusiastically suggested they change their plans and march north. Surely, this large lake had to be the source of the Nile.

Burton wouldn't hear of it. And as expedition leader, he had the final say.

Unrelated to that discussion, Burton then got very sick. He could not walk, or even stand. In fact, he would not walk unsupported for almost a year. "The whole body was palsied, powerless, motionless, and the limbs appeared to wither and die," he later wrote. The nameless condition persisted, and after weeks of suffering, his condition only grew worse. His hands and feet began to feel as if they were engulfed in flames. Speke feared that Burton was near death.

At the risk of sounding heartless, one has to ponder the very different life that John Hanning Speke would have enjoyed if Burton had simply died. Speke would have taken control of the expedition. The RGS had specifically ordered Burton and Speke to locate the lake at Ujiji and then travel northwest in search of the source. Speke would have done precisely that. He would have returned to London with maps pinpointing the source. There would have been no Nile Debate. No soul-searching afternoon of hunting on the eve of that great debate.

But Burton would live thirty-two more years. He would return to England, marry Isabel Arundel, set aside his Muslim leanings as an act of youthful indiscretion by converting to Catholicism, and be laid to rest in the cemetery at St. Mary Magdalen's Roman Catholic church in Mortlake, just outside London. His elaborate handcarved stone tomb would bear the design of a Bedouin tent, in which the coffins of Burton and Isabel would rest side by side for all eternity*—and where they can still be seen to this day, thanks to a viewing window and ladder around the back of the tomb.

11

Perhaps fearing that Speke would abandon him and complete the RGS mission all by himself, Burton summoned what can only be described as superhuman powers. He ordered that

*The 8-foot-tall tomb has recently been cleaned after years of neglect. Visitors are directed to walk around back, where the ladder leads up to a viewing window. The Burtons' coffins are clearly visible, if a little spooky.

the expedition leave the comforts of Kazeh and immediately make for Ujiji. Burton still couldn't walk, so a litter was fashioned and six porters were hired to carry him.

Speke had suffered his own share of illness, but his constitution was the sturdier of the two men. So it seems unfair, or at least bad luck, that he was struck by a bout of ophthalmia several weeks after setting out from Kazeh.

He could not have picked a worse time to lose his vision.

Ophthalmia is what happens when the eyes are subjected to day after day of intense glare and the retinas burn. This is why it is important to wear sunglasses. For Speke, the bloody eyes and inability to see came from the African sun. Christopher Columbus suffered this condition often, thanks to the glare bouncing off the sea, and it was said that his eyes bled. Burton, who also endured ophthalmia periodically, described it as "an almost total blindness, rendering every object enclouded as though by a misty veil."

Meanwhile, Burton's health was not much better than Speke's. The journey was growing so difficult that Burton was on the verge of turning back to Kazeh. The westward path was a continuum of swamps, dense jungle, and bamboo. Monsoon-force rains alternated with periods of scorching sun, making for constant daytime misery. Burton's carriers all ran off, stealing many of his possessions and losing his bedding. Speke's blindness made it impossible to travel on foot, forcing both men to depend upon donkeys as a mode of transportation.

So it was that on February 13, 1858, Burton and Speke

were both perched atop donkeys as the small remainders of their caravan marched up a rocky hill, past thorn trees, and through thick grass. A porter led Speke's animal. The donkey struggled with its burden and needed to be coaxed up the uneven climb. It finally reached the summit, only to collapse and die. Burton then ordered the group to stop and rest.

The expedition's goals appeared futile. There was no point in going on. To Burton, it made more sense to march back to Kazeh to convalesce, then try again to find the lakes of central Africa when he and Speke were completely healed.

Then Burton saw something shiny and silver far below. "What is that?" he asked Sidi Mubarak Bombay, his lead porter.*

"I believe it is the water," replied Bombay.

Both men knew what he meant. Not just any body of water, they were at long last gazing upon Tanganyika. Everyone, that is, except Speke.

The emotional significance of the moment overwhelmed

*Bombay was an African but got his unusual name after being sold into slavery as a young boy and taken away to India. Emancipated after his owner's death, Bombay returned to Africa and led expeditions for Burton, Speke, Stanley, and Verney Lovett Cameron, with whom he walked across Africa from east to west. In his lifetime he also followed the Nile from its source all the way to the Mediterranean. The RGS bestowed a silver medal for achievement on him in 1876. Nonetheless, he is still viewed as nothing more than a prolific load bearer rather than the man leading the way—which, in fact, he was. Based on the *explorare* etymology of explorer—one who goes ahead and cries out what he sees—Bombay is clearly one of history's greatest.

both of the Englishmen. Looking to the left and then to the right, Burton realized that the lake was so massive that it was impossible to see the north or south shores of Tanganyika.* The far bank looked to be 35 miles away.†

"Nothing," he later wrote, "could be more picturesque than this first view of the Tanganyika Lake, as it lay in the lap of the mountains, basking in the gorgeous tropical sunshine." He added descriptions of "zigzag" paths and emerald green hills, and of the gleaming yellow sands and small breaking waves.

Burton developed an immediate emotional connection to Lake Tanganyika. Thanks to Speke's temporary blindness, he was the first European to lay eyes upon it. It was a bond to which he would never let go. For the rest of his life, that body of water would be a source of pride to Richard Francis Burton. Tanganyika was *his* lake. The expedition reaching its shores was *his* accomplishment. Burton would barely see more of its shoreline than the village of Ujiji, and yet he would later expound one theory after another about its geography, as if he had circumnavigated each and every inch of his beloved lake's shoreline.

Burton would also convince himself of one other great truth: Lake Tanganyika was the source of the Nile River. It was a truth that Burton would soon defend with a fiery passion.

---

*The actual length is 418.2 miles, making it the longest lake on Earth.
†Actual width is 45 miles.

Speke didn't experience that emotional connection to Tanganyika. After seven long months on the trail he couldn't even see the shining blue waters, let alone feel passionate about it. If anything, he sulked. "The great lake in question was nothing but mist and glare before my eyes," he wrote despondently. "The lovely Tanganyika Lake could be seen in all its glory by everybody but myself."

With that, the Richard Burton Expedition gamely made their way down the mountain into Ujiji, where they arrived on February 14. Appropriately, this marked the seventy-ninth anniversary of the murder of Captain James Cook—the very death that propelled Britain from nautical exploration to land-based exploration, opening up the era of African discovery. If this was, indeed, The Source, the coincidence could not have been more profound.

Speke and Burton soon settled in for a rest in Ujiji, where they experienced even more of the luxury and abundance that they had experienced in Kazeh. Speke purchased a pair of stained glass spectacles at the Arab market to protect his eyes from the sun. Burton slept on the mud floor of their rented hut, slowly regaining his health. There was still much work to be done to fulfill their RGS orders, but making it to Ujiji was a significant milestone.

It can be argued that until this point in their journey Burton and Speke were merely wanderers—intrepid wanderers, but wanderers nonetheless, simply following in the footsteps of Arab slave traders. But Ujiji, that bustling town on the shores of Lake Tanganyika, with its bountiful markets and newly captured slaves, was where they were forced to blaze their own trails.

Curiosity and Hope were long ago specters in their rear-view mirrors. Passion had driven them from Zanzibar to Ujiji on a journey fraught with near death, blindness, ineptitude, and brilliant solutions to impossible problems.

Now it was time to step off into the unknown. For that, Burton and Speke would require a brand-new trait.

COURAGE

1

The US Department of State's website issues regular travel warnings that detail the world's most dangerous and unstable countries. The Democratic Republic of the Congo is a perpetual presence on that list, right up there with North Korea, Pakistan, and Libya. Those contemplating a trip to the Congo are told to be wary of everything from polio, cholera, and yellow fever to roving bands of militia. Public transport is to be avoided at all costs, police checkpoints often result in wrongful imprisonment, and stopping at the scene of an accident is strongly discouraged due to random acts of mob violence. There are few viable roads and railways through its hundreds of miles of rain forest. Walking outside after dark, taking photos of government officials and buildings, and roving gangs of street children are all to be avoided. Certain regions of the Congo are completely off-limits not only to tourists, but to embassy personnel as well. One such area, the State Department warns, is home to armed groups who "pillage, steal vehicles, kidnap, rape, kill, and carry out military or paramilitary operations in which civilians are indiscriminately targeted."

In other words, not a very nice place.

The Congo is on the western shore of Lake Tanganyika. Tanzania is on the eastern. Ujiji is no longer the main hub on that part of the lake, which means that ferry travel across to the Congo begins in nearby Kigoma. Technology in the form of Internet cafés and television have trickled into the heart of Africa, but even simple acts of commerce suggest that the encroachment of the modern world is slow in coming. There are no ATMs, and when I attempted to pay by credit card one storeowner examined my Visa from a number of different angles before asking, "Where is the money?"

Yet for all the dangers and lack of modernization, there is a great appeal to the coastline of Lake Tanganyika. Sunrise on a clear day is golden and inviting. Fishing boats can be seen arriving after a long night on the water. The people are friendly and eager to offer directions. As of this writing, there are no State Department travel warnings about Tanzania.

Burton and Speke experienced this same duality. On one side of Lake Tanganyika was prosperous Ujiji. There, merchants charged extortionist prices, and a damp lakeside climate rotted books and botanical specimens, but otherwise life was easy. The option of spending the day in an angle of repose constantly beckoned, making it the perfect stopover for two extremely sick explorers. "I lay a fortnight upon the earth," Burton wrote, "too blind to read or write."

On the far side of the lake were dense rain forests, hostile tribes, constant peril, and an utter lack of the convenient Arab footpath they had followed to Ujiji. Yet Burton and Speke needed to go across. The first step of their RGS mission had been to reach the lake region of central Africa. This had been accomplished. Now, before they could turn around and go home, Burton and Speke needed to recuperate, then find it within themselves to push into the unknown and explore the lake's perimeter. They needed to find the place where the Nile flowed northward out of the lake. The Arabs and the local tribes swore that such a river existed, though absolutely none of them had ever seen it. But the fact of the matter was simple: the truth about the Nile was out there.

Find that river, and Lake Tanganyika was the source. Fail to find that river, and the source sprung from someplace else.

In other words, sick as they were, Burton and Speke would be required to actually explore.

This is where courage enters the picture. It was the Greek philosopher Aristotle who noted that the definition of courage is twofold: (1) recognition that a cause is worthwhile; and (2) that an individual faces danger with the full knowledge of what the potential outcome might be. A soldier on the field of battle is considered courageous if he risks his life so that others may live. However, if that same individual suffers from impulsivity or manic behavior, he is behaving irrationally—not courageously.

That definition applies to physical courage, moral courage, and any other small daily act that requires a willful decision to accept a challenge, no matter how big or small. Courage is New York City firefighters climbing up into the twin towers on September 11. Courage is also the child who asks that the training wheels be taken off his or her two-wheeled bicycle. Researchers don't use the word "courage" when describing this process. They call the object of peril a "decision point" and the act of behaving courageously as "overcoming fear."

Because the ability to be courageous is not just learned but also accrued—decision by decision, challenge by challenge, throughout our lives—that youthful day those firemen chose to take off their training wheels would form the basis of their heroism so many years later. Researchers refer to this process as "making fear-overriding decisions over time."

But almost all of us learn to ride a bike. Not everyone, however, possesses the courage to walk into a burning skyscraper when everyone else is racing out. Why do some of us acquire a deep well of bravery while others rarely if ever venture outside their comfort zone?

In a word: mediocrity. Just as courage is a willful act to confront risk, so mediocrity is a choice to avoid risk. Once again, we have our lizard brain to thank for this. It kicks in whenever it sniffs a fearful situation, reminding us that the propagation of the species depends upon risk avoidance, no matter how milquetoast—or even cowardly—our behavior might appear.

This instigates a bodily reaction known as somatic arousal. Our heart rate increases immediately, because the large muscles of the legs will need extra oxygen when the order is given to run away. This is also why we breathe faster in pressure situations—the lungs take in extra oxygen and immediately shunt it into the bloodstream.

The adrenal glands, which are just above the kidneys, then secrete adrenaline and other defensive hormones into the bloodstream. Memory pathways in the brain are instantly enhanced, so that we remember the situation more vividly than a less dangerous event.* The stress hormones also trigger excess perspiration, leading to the clammy palms and notorious "cold sweat" so often associated with being afraid. They also cause the hairs on our arms to stand up. These "goose bumps," as we know them, are medically known as piloerection, and serve no modern purpose. It has been theorized that it made prehistoric man—who had far more hair covering his body—

---

*The brain does not record all events with the same clarity of memory. It would appear that the enhanced memory of a fearful event would be to prevent an individual from repeating it. When an event becomes too traumatic, the brain often distorts this memory, perhaps as a coping mechanism.

look bigger when approached by a predator. It's worth noting that cats also display piloerection in times of fear.

All that blood and oxygen rushing to our legs causes an increase in muscle tension. This is why our knees shake when we're afraid.

And finally, a portion of the brain stem known as the pontine micturition center is bombarded by electronic signals, demanding that it do its job. That particular and highly specialized job is to control the bladder. This is why many human beings react to fear the same way as gazelles, pigeons, laboratory rats, and many other members of the animal kingdom: by peeing all over themselves.

Thank goodness for courage.

A portion of the brain known as the subgenual anterior cingulate cortex (sgACC) analyzes the fear and decides whether it is a true life-and-death threat, or merely a burst of anxiety. The heart rate and breathing slow down, the legs stop shaking, the clammy hands go dry, and we don't feel embarrassing warmth running down our legs. The most marvelous thing about the sgACC is that it can bring about this sense of calm even when a threat is very real. A lifetime of courageous decisions sharpens the sgACC, making it easier and easier to override the lizard brain in dangerous situations.* For this very reason, elite commando outfits such as the British Special Air

---

*Sometimes we place too much emphasis on the wrong fears. For instance, the odds of death by snake bite is 1 in 145 million. The odds of death by heart disease? 1 in 400.

Service (SAS) train using live ammunition. The danger is still all too real, but the brain learns to differentiate between gunfire that will kill and a shot too far away to do harm.

The sgACC's ability to stop somatic arousal is not only instantaneous, but can occur before we realize we're in danger. The brain is capable of making decisions six to seven seconds before we are aware that one is required. Which means that we choose whether to be courageous or cowardly before consciously making the decision to do so.

2

"Courage," wrote the academic and theologian C. S. Lewis, "is not simply one of the virtues, but the form of every virtue at the testing point." Yet as much as we admire acts of courage, there is also an institutionalized embrace of mediocrity in the modern world. Settling for good enough is rampant, and widely encouraged. Curiosity, for instance, that great trait that starts all voyages of discovery (personal and otherwise), is actively suppressed. "Curiosity killed the cat" is such a common phrase that we overlook its crystal clear subtext: "Don't take risks." Or, in corporate-speak: "Don't think outside the box."

The French aviator Antoine de Saint-Exupéry once wrote of a commute on the morning he was about to make his very first flight. The city bus was filled with clerks, bankers, and laborers. "I heard them talking to one another in murmurs and whispers. They talked about illness, money, and shabby domestic cares. Their talk painted the walls of the dismal prison in which these men had locked themselves up. And suddenly I had a vision of the face of destiny," Saint-Exupéry noted.

Then, enraged at lives not being lived to their fullest, he directed his writing to the mediocrity surrounding him. "You rolled yourself into a ball in your genteel security, in routine, raising a modest rampart against the winds and the tides and the stars. You have chosen not to be perturbed by great problems, having trouble enough to forget your own fate as a man. Nobody grasped you by the shoulders while there was still time. Now the clay of which you were shaped has dried and hardened, and naught in you will ever awaken the sleeping musician, the poet, the astronomer that possibly inhabited you in the beginning."

The hardening that Saint-Exupéry mentions is born out of mankind's cultural embrace of mediocrity. This herd mentality is seen in everything from popular hairstyles to clothing to music—emphasis on the word "popular." Parents want to see their children succeed in life, and know that going along with the crowd seems to be the best way to make that possible.

"All men dream, but not equally," wrote T. E. Lawrence, the legendary British desert explorer, making a distinction between those who choose mediocrity and those who choose courage. "Those who dream by night in the dusty recesses of their minds wake in the day to find that it was vanity. But the dreamers of the day are dangerous men, for they may act on their dreams with open eyes, to make them possible."

Inspiring as those words might be, children are not raised to be those "dreamers of the day." Daydreaming,* in fact, is widely viewed as a lazy waste of time. Throughout their schooling years, it is made clear that children who choose to simply do as they are told, rather than those who challenge conventional wisdom through an unconventional creative thought process, will be amply rewarded for their acquiescence. The educational system, corporate culture, and most every aspect of modern life are comfortable with the status quo, resenting and fearing anything that introduces radical change. Men such as the firefighters marching into those twin towers and the navy SEALs who shot Osama bin Laden most likely did not learn that courage-producing continuum of "fear-overriding decisions" from their teachers, high school sports coaches, or not even their parents. Instead, it was their years of rigid professional training that provided them with calm detachment in the face of danger.

Their commitment to their comrades—"brothers" in the words of New York City firefighters—adds an ethical aspect known as moral courage. Those with high levels of moral development are driven by their conscience to do the right

*We all daydream; some of us just hide it better. A Harvard study of 2,250 subjects showed that their minds were wandering an average of 47 percent of the time. There is a close correlation between daydreaming and creative problem-solving, which is why a long run or shower tends to aid the creative thought process. It's worth noting that the only activity to which the subjects of the study committed complete and total focus was lovemaking.

thing at all times. Personal experience, professional training, a lifetime of knowledge acquisition, and the surrounding environment combine with this reliance on moral values to empower individuals in the face of danger. Among others, this moral courage is seen in the nurse who acts as an advocate for her patient, the civil rights activist, the whistle blower, and first responders such as firefighters, smoke jumpers, and police.

It would be a stretch to consider the explorers highly moral. Many, such as the pirate William Dampier,* had few morals whatsoever, and were entirely motivated by money. But by its very nature, the profession of explorer involved traveling alone into places with ways and beliefs different from anything they'd ever experienced. An explorer had two ethical choices in such an environment: rely on his conscience as a moral compass, or compromise his morals to suit his surroundings. Jack Speke, for instance, once watched an infant being boiled alive in Africa. Yet he did nothing to stop it, a fact greeted with widespread horror when news of the atrocity reached England.

Perhaps the most famous example of physical and moral courage in the annals of exploration is that of Lawrence Oates,

*An Englishman, Dampier circumnavigated the globe three times, explored Western Australia, and rescued Alexander Selkirk (the inspiration for Robinson Crusoe) from the Pacific island where he'd been stranded. Jonathan Swift mentions him by name in *Gulliver's Travels*. He also introduced the words barbecue, avocado, subspecies, and chopsticks to the English language.

a British cavalry officer who traveled to the South Pole as part of Robert Falcon Scott's 1910–12 Terra Nova expedition.

If ever a complete absence of morality exists on the face of the Earth, it is at that barren wasteland of snow, ice, wind, and horrific freezing temperatures known as the South Pole. It is, in a word, awful. At the time of Scott's expedition, no man had ever set foot upon it, and no tribes of indigenous people had developed a religion to explain the power that the weather and terrain had over their lives. It was a blank slate of morality—which did absolutely nothing to detract from mankind's desperate desire to see the pole, touch the pole, and breathe, if only for a short time, its frozen air.

Scott's goal was to be the first. En route from England to Antarctica, he learned that a Norwegian expedition would be attempting the same journey. Led by Roald Amundsen, the taciturn discoverer of the Northwest Passage, they were a well-disciplined team. Amundsen was known for being rigid and almost heartless in the way he drove his men. Scott's compassion, on the other hand, was legendary. He accepted frailties in other men that he found so despicable in himself.

Rather than make much of the race to the pole, and perhaps endanger the lives of his men, Scott chose to downplay the rivalry with Amundsen. "The proper, as well as the wiser, course is for us to proceed as though this had not happened. To go forward and do our best for the honor of our country without fear or panic. There is no doubt that Amundsen's plan is a very serious menace to ours," he wrote.

Scott and his team set off across the Ross Ice Shelf on November 1, 1911. Amundsen was already two weeks into his journey. Scott's supplies were carried by dogs, Siberian ponies, and motor vehicles on tracks. All but the dogs gave out within a few days.

As one can imagine, the journey was horrid. "Polar exploration is at once the cleanest and most isolated way of having a bad time which has been devised" was how Antarctic explorer Apsley Cherry-Gerrard described the expedition. He shivered so hard on that trip that his teeth shattered from all the chattering.

The Age of Polar Exploration was anticipated by Aristotle, who theorized that the world needed a set of balanced land-masses on either end to spin properly. The fringes of the Arctic were explored first, by Vikings and other sailors, due to their proximity to Europe. But the Age of Polar Exploration was never fully addressed until the discovery of Antarctica by Captain James Cook in 1775, which confirmed Aristotle's theory. It had long been fantasized that the South Pole was a place of great jewels and riches, but even when it became apparent that it consisted of absolutely nothing but snow and ice, mining its nonexistent riches was replaced by the manic desire to touch its geographic soul—the 90°, 0° mark on the map.

The same was true of the equally awful North Pole. Which is ironic, because for the longest time, mankind had absolutely no inclination to chart the polar regions. It wasn't until the nineteenth century that the first expedition of substance was undertaken, by British naval officer William Parry in 1827. He attempted to reach the North Pole, but failed. He did, however, succeed in reaching 82 degrees north latitude, a record that stood for forty-nine years.*

Polar exploration was not as glamorous as finding the source of the Nile, walking across Australia's outback, charting the North American continent, or climbing the great Mount Everest. But by the end of the nineteenth century the first three achievements on that list had been accomplished, and the fourth appeared to be as physically impossible as swimming to the bottom of the ocean. It can almost be said that mankind only reluctantly began racing to the poles because all the warm destinations had already been reached.

As we've established, there is nothing at the North or the South Pole. Nothing. Yet men endured some of exploration's greatest miseries and calamities for the privilege of standing on perhaps the two loneliest spots on the planet. They bundled themselves in layer upon layer of clothing—reindeer-skin boots and pants wrapped in windproof canvas, reindeer-skin gloves, waterproof canvas smocks—and beneath it all, itchy wool sweaters, hats, and underwear that became soaked in sweat from their exertions, and then froze the instant the explorers stopped moving. They began each journey with sled dogs. By design, their beloved animal companions were then

*Parry's enduring legacy was the introduction of canned food to polar exploration.

killed and eaten whenever food grew sparse. And as if all that
wasn't bad enough, polar explorers endured diseases such as
scurvy that were once consigned to sea travel, and even lead
poisoning from poorly soldered cans of food.

All this, just to say they'd been the first to stand on a
90°, 0° point on the map.

Strangely, once the poles had been reached, polar exploration was done. Complete. Nobody wanted to go back. What
was the point?* It was the ultimate example of exploration
as competition, and one of the rare times in history that being
first mattered most—and being second, not at all.

It was Scott's route that proved his undoing. His ascent
of the Beardmore Glacier took valuable time and drained his
supplies. Scott's team was just 178 miles from the Pole when
Amundsen arrived first on December 14, 1911. By the time
Scott descended the glacier and reached the South Pole on
January 18, 1912, he and his team were greeted by the dispir-
iting sight of a small tent on the exact spot. Inside the tent was
a Norwegian flag. A depressed Scott was devastated. "Great
God! This is an awful place, and terrible enough for us to have
labored to it without the reward of priority."

Scott's first impulse was to withdraw into his depression,
yet he realized that his actions would have grave effects on
the morale of his men. The lot of them were already suffering

*The 1958 Commonwealth Trans-Antarctic Expedition was led by none
other than Mount Everest climber Sir Edmund Hillary.

from scurvy, frostbite, and exhaustion after months battling the –40° temperatures. Scott set aside his disappointment and rallied the men for the journey back to the Ross Ice Shelf.

They reached Beardmore Glacier on February 7, during a windstorm. After taking time to collect rock samples, including some with plant impressions that proved the land had once been forested, they continued. On February 17, Seaman Edgar Evans died a short distance from the supply camp they had established on the glacier.

Food was dwindling and the distance to travel was still great, but Scott was the very model of composure. Then things got worse. Just 31 miles from a depot containing a ton of supplies, Scott was forced by serious blizzards to halt their progress. It was there that army captain Lawrence Oates, afflicted with a mind-boggling case of frostbite, gave in to despair. The blizzard would not cease. By that time the dogs had all been eaten and the other food stores were gone, too.

The key to staying alive meant reaching the cache of canned food they had stored on their outbound journey. But Oates was suffering from scurvy and his feet were completely frostbitten. At night he slept with one leg outside his reindeer-skin sleeping bag so that it would freeze and thus kill the pain in his toes. There was no way Oates could continue, and no way for Scott or the others to carry him. So when a blizzard once again pinned the expedition inside their tents on March 16, 1912, Oates knew what had to be done. "I am just going outside and may be some time," he said to his companions, who knew full well he was about to sacrifice his life for theirs.

So it was that Oates opened the tent flap and stepped out into the blizzard.

This, in the words of another polar explorer, is what he encountered: "There is something extravagantly insensate about an Antarctic blizzard," wrote Admiral Richard Byrd. "Its vindictiveness cannot be measured on an anemometer sheet. It is more than just a wind, it is a solid wall of snow moving at gale force, pounding like surf. The whole malevolent rush is focused upon you as a personal enemy. In the senseless explosion of sound you are reduced to a crawling thing on the margin of the disintegrating world; you can't see, you can't hear, you can hardly move."

Imagine the arc of Oates's exploration: curiosity, hope, and passion got him to the South Pole. Courage allowed him to face the very real fact that his injuries would be the death of his companions. Independence opened that tent flap. Self-discipline quieted the voice in his head that told him to turn right back around and dive back into that reindeer skin sleeping bag. And finally, perseverance told him to keep staggering farther and farther into the blizzard until the cold finally shut his body down for good. Maybe he opened his coat to speed the process. But he walked, and kept on walking, until the end finally came.

This much we know, because Oates's body has never been found.

Sadly, Oates's efforts were in vain. The rest of Scott's expedition perished within two weeks. A blizzard trapped them in their tent just days after Oates died. Food ran out before the storm ended.

Evidence shows that Scott was the last to freeze to death, because even with his dead mates lying on either side of him, he wrote a series of letters and journal entries detailing the bravery and bad luck his expedition endured. "Every day now we have been ready to start for our depot eleven miles away, but outside the door of the tent, it remains a scene of swirling snowdrift. I do not think we can hope for any better things now," he wrote on March 29, 1912. "I do not think we can hope for any better things now. We shall see it to the end, but we are getting weaker, of course. It seems a pity, but I do not think I can write more. For God's sake, look after our people."

Scott's letters are how the world learned of Oates. Otherwise, that selfless act would have gone unknown. "With the blizzard at its height," wrote Scott, "he left the tent and was never seen again."

The bodies of Scott, Edward Wilson, and Henry Bowers were discovered on November 12, 1912, side by side in their tent, where they had slowly died from starvation and cold. Given the choice to commit suicide by injecting themselves with the copious amounts of morphine in their medical kit, they opted to endure the agony of slowly freezing to death. This is an extreme form of moral courage, choosing to die naturally rather than by their own hand because it was against their personal principles, even though absolutely no one but themselves and their Maker would ever know the truth.

Scott, Wilson, and Bowers were left where they were found. Their tent was collapsed upon them and snow allowed to accumulate, burying the bodies forever. The cold has no doubt preserved them without decomposition. So the three of them lie there still, side by side by side.

In the century since his death, the location of Scott's tent has been lost. Yet because his party died atop frozen ocean rather than land, their journey is not yet complete. The inexorable movement of ice away from the Antarctic landmass toward the Southern Ocean means that someday their bodies will be part of an ice floe that will drift and eventually melt, giving their bodies up to the sea.

3

So how to develop such a profound reservoir of courage? For the explorers, it meant the daily discipline of confronting each and every challenge head-on. The first step of every journey was always the hardest. Each day would bring failure, surprise, and maybe even death. Their trick was to be bold, even when they were cold, wet, tired, hungry, miserable, or sick. This didn't mean explorers had more courage that other segments of society lacked. They simply believed it was better to try and fail than not to try at all. "A hero is no braver than an ordinary man," wrote Ralph Waldo Emerson. "He is just braver five minutes longer."

A most unlikely example of this daily discipline was botanist Alexander von Humboldt. Entitled, chubby, and gay, the German socialite's only enduring interests were his mother and the study of botany. Yet he undertook two of the most courageous journeys in history.

Humboldt was born in 1769, the same year that Isabel Godin began her long journey down the Amazon in search of her husband. He was the son of a wealthy Prussian cavalry officer and a French Huguenot woman who had fled to Berlin to escape religious persecution. His father died when he was ten. By 1790, Alexander von Humboldt seemed destined to spend his lifetime squandering his somewhat sizable inheritance when fate intervened in rather cruel fashion. First, he traveled extensively through Europe with Georg Forster, who had sailed aboard Captain Cook's second voyage of discovery as a young man.

Though Humboldt was fifteen years younger than Forster, the two shared a passion for travel that inspired Humboldt to pursue new adventures. Then Humboldt's mother died just days after being diagnosed with breast cancer. Alone for the first time in his life, he consoled himself by pursuing a long-stifled yearning for international travel. Humboldt soon met Aimé Bonpland, a young French doctor who shared his unlikely passion for plants and animals. The two became fast friends. When the Napoleonic Wars put an end to their goal of exploring the Nile together, they came up with an audacious plan to explore the jungles of South America, which were thought to be full of new and exotic plants. To see if they were cut out for the journey they walked the 500 miles from Marseilles to Madrid together. Their journey ended at Spain's royal palace, where they sought an audience with King Carlos IV in the hopes that he would grant them permission to explore his nation's South American colonies. Disregarding the obvious fact that Humboldt and Bonpland had no practical botany experience, Carlos not only met with them, but he was so mesmerized by their profound curiosity that he put them on the next ship to Cumaná. The journey had begun.

On February 7, 1800, Humboldt and Bonpland set out on foot from Caracas, planning to trace the Orinoco River from the ocean backward to where it connected with the Amazon. Along the way they would observe and catalog whatever plants and animals they might see. When Christopher Columbus had discovered the Orinoco in 1498 he thought it was the great river that was reputed to flow out of Eden. It was conceivable that every type of plant and animal would be found there. Though they didn't think that true, Humboldt and Bonpland had chosen the most symbolically powerful journey in all of botany to make their exploration debut. The two men must have needed all the courage they possessed to even consider such a challenge.

It was a journey that had never been attempted before, and the likelihood of success by the two inexperienced, pampered adventurers seemed slim. The heat and humidity were stifling and the physical discomforts prohibitive, ranging from insects that ate their flesh to an electric fish they encountered when wading the swampy llanos grassland. This *Eletrophorus electricus*, as named by Humboldt, produced a current of 650 volts—enough to kill a horse. Humboldt personally allowed the fish to jolt him so that he might experience this phenomenon. "The shock," he wrote, "produced a violent pain in the knees, and in almost every joint for the rest of the day."

By April the two were deeper into the Orinoco Basin than any previous explorers. When their rowboat gave out, they purchased dugout canoes from local tribes, then paddled farther and farther upriver. They made their beds each night along the river's edge, exposed to insects, poisonous snakes, and jaguars. The slightest cut became a running sore. Worst of all to the would-be botanists, the humidity destroyed their notebooks, making it impossible to keep detailed scientific records. Yet they pushed on. Each day saw new discoveries.

After traveling more than 1,500 miles upriver, Humboldt and Bonpland discovered the Casiquiare Canal, a natural channel linking the Orinoco and the Rio Negro. Recognizing that the latter river fed into the Amazon, Humboldt proclaimed their three-month journey a success. He had personally collected twelve thousand new varieties of plants. That celebration was quickly cut short, however, on the eve of their return when both men were stricken by typhoid from drinking untreated water. Weak, burning with fever, and doubled over with stomach pains, they set out for home, knowing that it was imperative to get to a hospital. When Bonpland's condition worsened until he was near death, his body covered in rose-colored splotches and the pain of his constant stomach cramps made worse by migraine headaches, it was Humboldt who paddled their dugout down the rapids and swamps of the Orinoco. After an entire month of this determined suffering, their painful odyssey came to an end when they reached the town of Angostura.*

Both men spent six months in the hospital. Word of their journey soon traveled back to Europe, where they were widely viewed as heroes. Humboldt and Bonpland had metamorphosed from dreamers to a pair of truly courageous (and famous) explorers. Thus, rather than sail home and bask in the limelight, both men were hungry to push their limits once again.

They immediately traveled to Cartagena, and began a journey up the uncharted Magdalena River. It took them six weeks to reach the city of Bogotá. When they came to the point where they could go no farther, Humboldt and Bonpland purchased mules to help them cross the Andes. As they trudged through the deep snows of Quindiu Pass, Humboldt was inspired by the sight of a distant peak. The young German had never attempted mountain climbing before, but was determined to attain that majestic summit. Unknowingly, he and Bonpland were about to become the first mountain climbers in South American history.

*The original home of Angostura bitters, a concentrated mix of alcohol and spices still used to flavor drinks and food.

The mountain was Chimborazo. At 20,564 feet the snow-covered volcano is one of the highest peaks in the Southern Hemisphere. The first portion of the climb was relatively uneventful, but once they came within a mile of the summit, Humboldt and Bonpland encountered obstacle after obstacle: snow, ice, low clouds. The altitude made them nauseous, and they began to bleed from the eyes, lips, and gums. Still, they pressed on. But just below the summit the two explorers came across a vast ravine that lay between them and the top that was impossible to cross. Despite the fact that they didn't make the summit, the altitude they attained was the highest point anyone in the world had ever climbed to that time. It would be thirty years before that record was broken.

The rest of that 1801–2 journey was one form of exploration after another: Observing the transit of the planet Venus across the face of the sun in Lima; investigating Incan ruins at Canar (the first archaeological expedition in South America); and collecting specimens of bark from the cinchona tree, the antimalarial source of quinine. When it was done, they accepted an invitation to visit President Thomas Jefferson at his home in Virginia, where Humboldt spent three months perusing the great man's library before sailing for Europe, where he lived in comfort and splendor for the rest of his long life.*

*With the exception of a journey across Russia, that was the end of Humboldt's exploration career. He died in Berlin at age eighty-nine.

It could be said that spending the final sixty years of his life basking in praise and adulation was Humboldt's reward for those years of daily courage in the wilds of South America. His journey's ultimate conclusion was an explorer's wet dream: undertake a great adventure, complete it with smashing thoroughness and success, return home alive and in good health, be acknowledged with a lifetime of wealth and fame, and then live on after death through the various places and species christened in his honor. In addition to the Humboldt Current, a rough count shows forty-seven cities, schools, plants, sea creatures, and animals named for Humboldt. These include a squid, penguin, orchid, skunk, and a gorgeous yellow flower from the Ultricularia genus known as a bladderwort.*

4

Nothing and no place is named after Sir Richard Francis Burton. Mount Speke in Uganda, Speke Gulf in Tanzania, and a very small creature known as the Speke's gazelle are all that bear the name of John Hanning Speke. This is not to say that they wouldn't have been interested in the enduring

---

*The world leader in naming places was Captain Cook, whose charting of the Pacific allowed him to name hundreds of bays, islands, capes, and heads. A very large proportion are named for either King George III, the British monarch at the time of his voyages; George's wife, Charlotte; or various officials in British government at that time. A Latinization of the monarch's name gives us *Georgia*, as in South Georgia Island, to which Ernest Shackleton so famously sailed in his open boat.

fame Humboldt enjoyed—after all, Burton and Speke were two men of considerable ego. But gazelles and bladderworts weren't their primary focus. Their expedition was always bent on a bigger legacy. Burton was a keen ethnographer and studious in collecting botanical samples. Speke was also enthralled with new discoveries in plants and animals. So once they found Lake Tanganyika—a great accomplishment in its own right—the journey then focused solely on finding the source of the Nile. Nothing else mattered. Dick Burton and Jack Speke were on the verge of solving history's greatest puzzle. Let Humboldt, now living out his final years in Berlin, have his plants and penguin. Let George Everest have the world's tallest mountain. Let Livingstone spend years and years fixated on the Zambezi River—important in its own way, but nowhere nearly as mythic as the source.

If only in Britain, and its obsession with all things Nile, Burton and Speke would be immortal.

Which may explain why Speke got a little antsy once he could see again. Burton, with his own blindness and paralysis, was slipping closer to death, and Speke was eager to explore the far side of Lake Tanganyika. On March 3, after consulting with Burton, Speke and a small complement of the caravan boarded a dugout canoe to make the crossing. The journey could not have been comfortable. Twenty-three men were crammed into the long, flimsy wooden craft, including an interpreter, a cook, two armed Baluchi guards for protection, and eighteen paddlers. As anyone who has ever traveled by canoe can attest, no sitting position in this cramped world of knees, elbows, and hard seats remained comfortable for long. Reclining, with so many bodies in such a confined space, was out of the question. Speke's only solace was his pipe, which he silently sat and smoked while keeping a sharp eye for the crocodiles that were fond of climbing into canoes and hauling men away.*

Inclement weather restricted their travel to the shore-line for the first few days, but the party finally made it across to the other side on March 8. The locals turned out to be friendly, if slightly fearful of a lone traveler, for such men were often slavers. One night while sleeping, Speke suffered the indignity of a beetle boring deeply into his ear, scratching its way deeper and deeper into his skull. Poking a finger into his auditory canal to flush out the insect only pushed the beetle in deeper. Speke then poured hot butter into the orifice, which had no effect. Spearing the beetle with the sharp tip of his knife finally killed the insect, but also punctured Speke's inner ear. The wound soon became infected, causing his face to become covered in boils. The hole in his ear would not heal for seven months, causing temporary deafness and a whistling sound every time Speke blew his nose. Legs and wings and other beetle body parts would emigrate out of the opening for

---

*They are still very much a danger. One mythic crocodile of this region has been named Gustave. Researchers who have tried to capture him estimate that Gustave is 60 feet long, weighs 1 ton, and is 60 years old. As of 2008, it was estimated he had eaten 300 humans.

almost a year. Speke would later refer to this random attack as some of the greatest pain he had ever known.

Yet Speke pushed on, trying his best to explore the lake in search of the mysterious river leading north.

But he failed. Making matters worse, when Speke returned to Ujiji after almost four weeks with nothing to show for his time and hardship, Burton not only mocked him for having achieved very little, but also made sure to write it up in his journal so he could once again publicly skewer Speke upon its publication.

The fact remained that they had to find that mysterious river. Burton was still not healed, but on April 9 he joined Speke for a second attempt. He was dragged to the lake and placed inside a dugout. What followed was a miserable adventure. Torrential rains pelted them daily. The men hired as paddlers smoked a great deal of cannabis, which brought about sleepiness and lack of motivation. Burton's tongue began to swell from severe ulcers. Crocodiles, mosquitoes, malaria, and cannibals along the shoreline (some who were known to prefer men roasted, and others known to eat them raw) were constant threats. There were villages along the coast so fierce that not even Arab slavers paid a visit. Finally, when Burton and Speke were literally hours away from the long-sought river, they put ashore to rest. There, the sons of a local chieftain informed them that this river—the Rusizi, as it is known—flowed *into* Lake Tanganyika, not out of it. Clearly, this could not be the source.

One would imagine that if an individual had walked half-way across Africa, enduring as many hardships and setbacks as Burton, that he would order the paddlers to travel just six short more hours up the shoreline so he could see the Rusizi's flow for himself. There was always a chance that the chieftain's sons were wrong, or that they were trying to keep white men from paddling there to capture slaves.

But Burton's famous reservoir of fearlessness had run dry. The man who boldly infiltrated the brothels of Karachi, the holy city of Mecca, and allowed himself to be held prisoner in Harar, now wanted no part of the Rusizi. Henry Morton Stanley, who would undertake this same journey twenty years later, would write that the instant Burton gave the order to turn around, his "struggle for the mastery over African geography ceased."

When pressed to explain himself later in London, Burton would insist that he lacked enough cloth and beads to finish the task. These were the standard form of currency in Africa, used for everything from payment for food to safe passage through a tribal homeland. At this point in the journey, Burton would argue, he barely had enough of these precious items to make it home. This was true. However, by a stroke of good luck, an Arab trader in Kazeh had thoughtfully sent a fresh shipment of cloth and beads to Ujiji. It arrived just before Burton and Speke began their return trip to civilization. Burton could have easily resupplied and continued his quest for the Nile. By then, however, he was done.

The US Navy SEALs force those who want to quit their rigorous basic training (BUDS—Basic Underwater Demolition School) to ring a ship's bell three times. Many times, as young men come to the end of their rope and reach for this bell, the school's instructors encourage them to rethink what they are about to do. Once that bell has been rung, it can't be unrung. The individual has then quit, and is no longer a viable candidate to be a SEAL.

Many would-be SEALs rethink their decision. Yet almost all of those who initially change their mind about ringing the bell later come back to once again tug on the clapper three times. They quit. The SEALs believe that when an individual comes to the conclusion that giving up is an option, there's no turning back. This is the opposite of choosing courage. And whether through fatigue, cold, starvation, pain, illness, homesickness, or any of a number of reasons, they give in to their fears. Their minds transition away from managing the discomfort of their rigorous training and begin to imagine how good it will feel when the discomfort ends.

Soon enough, it does.

5

This is precisely what happened to Burton. He was lame and often blind. His tongue had been covered in so many ulcers that he couldn't speak. The waters of Lake Tanganyika are not suitable for drinking or bathing by humans, given the preponderance of helminth parasites that cause an infection known as schistosomiasis, and yet Burton's chief complaint during the three-week canoe journey was that the paddlers kept splashing water on him. So he could have very well picked up that disease.

Any of a number of other illnesses, such as dengue fever, leishmaniasis, onchocerciasis, and filariasis could also have been responsible for his lethargy and inability to see (onchocerciasis is also known as river blindness). His effectiveness as an explorer was minimal, because he wasn't ambulatory. And the days of eating, drinking, and sleeping in Ujiji might have been a welcome respite when they first arrived, but a man of Burton's rapacious intellectual thirst would have grown bored after months of having nothing to read, write, or accomplish.

A "strange, inexplicable melancholy" began to haunt Burton. Africa's verdant landscape no longer enchanted him, and he began to long for his favorite haunts of Egypt and Arabia and the "rare simplicity of the desert."

Mentally, physically, and emotionally, Dick Burton was finished. This is not what he would tell the RGS upon his return to London, but it's precisely what happened. In fact, he would lie about his reasons for returning home before completing his mission, explaining to Sir Roderick Murchison, "I was compelled by want of supplies to desist from exploration."

The truth of the matter is that Dick Burton quit.

Speke, however, was not ready to give up.

He was eager to return to the Rusizi to confirm the direction of its flow. But the choice was not his to make. On May 26, 1858, at Burton's order, he and Speke turned their backs on Lake Tanganyika and began the long trip home to London.

Ironically, the British capital was a potentially more lethal place than the heart of Africa at that very moment, thanks to an overwrought city sewage system that would soon see the Thames overflowing with untreated waste and the city reeking of fecal matter in the hot summer sun, giving it a *mal aria* on par with vulgar Zanzibar—and far transcending the pristine air of the African savanna.

But there's no place like home, and with no way of knowing that London would soon have the potential to become the source of an enormous cholera outbreak, the Speke and Burton Expedition began the long march back to civilization.

Burton planned that they would lay over in Kazeh along the way to regain their health once and for all. Hearing this, Speke realized he might have one last chance to go see the northern lake he had been told of earlier. He quietly schemed to make a trip north to explore that other great inland sea they had heard about. "If you are not well enough when we reach Kazeh," he suggested to Burton, "I will go myself, and you can employ this time taking notes from the traveled Arabs."

This sentence must have been spoken delicately.

Speke was requesting to depart from the caravan and undertake a solitary exploration. It was also a veiled insult. While Speke was eager to see for himself whether the northern lake existed, Burton was content to write down the secondhand accounts of the Arabs who claimed to have seen it. It was Speke who tracked game, drew maps, and followed the nightly stars to accurately assess longitude—activities commensurate with exploration. With the exception of their soggy three-week canoe trip up the shoreline of Lake Tanganyika, Burton's major contributions to the journey since he laid eyes upon the lake were detailed ethnological observations about African tribes and customs.

But Burton was no longer interested in exploration by the time Speke made his request. He had become a traveler, a man on the outside looking in, eager to be home. This is not to denigrate the hardships and misery Burton had endured, nor to minimize his achievements. By the time the expedition arrived in Kazeh on June 20, 1858, he'd been in Africa for a year. He had every right to look forward to a rendezvous with Isabel rather than more sickness, blindness, paralysis, and misfortune.

Burton's supporters are legion, even today, and far more numerous than those of the less glamorous Speke. Biographers write of Burton's rage and passion, glamorizing his eccentricities and ignoring the very obvious fact that his greatest days as an explorer were already behind him when Speke asked if he might set off alone to investigate the northern lake. But Burton was done with Africa. Upon his return to London, he would begin a new career as a diplomat, forever turning his back on the man he had once been.

By their very nature, the seven traits of the explorers are a reminder to keep pushing, always. The lofty and impossible nature of their business left ample room for compromise, as seen by Burton. He had accomplished a lot, and had drawn some informed conclusions. As Speke stood before him, asking whether he might travel northward for a short period to investigate this uncharted lake, it was easy to rationalize that that was probably good enough. After all, Burton had found Lake Tanganyika.

But he hadn't finished the job. The RGS's orders had explicitly stated that the expedition was to travel northward from Lake Tanganyika to ensure that a northward-flowing river connected with the Nile.

I would suggest that Burton felt more than a little sheepish about the crisis of courage that prevented him from taking the time to heal, rather than traveling north with Speke. He would have some explaining to do in London. Nonetheless, Burton reluctantly agreed to let Speke leave Kazeh and search for the northern lake.

6

On July 9, 1858, still a little deaf and occasionally blind from his damaged retinas, John Hanning Speke marched north from Kazeh with a thirty-four-man caravan. He was known as "Mzungu"—the white man—to his porters and to the villagers he would meet along the way.

Speke walked north for three weeks. The landscape was dry and forested. The nights and early mornings were crisp and cold, even in the midst of summer. Speke's Victorian clothing, felt hat, pale skin, and light brown hair were invariably the subjects of much scrutiny when he entered a new village. The daily peril was hardly less than anywhere else in Africa he'd been so far. Speke grew so tired of explaining to locals why he would do something as "stupid as to go through danger and discomfort" needlessly that he invented the explanation that he was off in search of hippopotamus teeth.

There was a lightheartedness to Speke's solitary travel that hadn't previously existed. It was as if he were back in the wilds of India and Nepal on a solo hunting trip. But this was even better. Speke was having the adventure of his life and was in no hurry to return home. He simply kept walking farther and farther north, hoping that reports of a great lake were true.

They were. On August 3, John Hanning Speke discovered the source of the Nile.

Sort of.

INDEPENDENCE

It is not the critic who counts; not the man who points out how the strong man stumbles, or where the doer of deeds could have done them better. The credit belongs to the man who is actually in the arena, whose face is marred by dust and sweat and blood; who strives valiantly; who errs, who comes short again and again, because there is no effort without error and shortcoming; but who does actually strive to do the deeds; who knows great enthusiasms, the great devotions; who spends himself in a worthy cause; who at the best knows in the end the triumph of high achievement, and who at the worst, if he fails, at least fails while daring greatly, so that his place shall never be with those cold and timid souls who neither know victory nor defeat.

—Teddy Roosevelt, "Citizenship in
a Republic," April 23, 1910

1

The true source of the world's longest river, as ascertained in 2006 by a team of adventurers known as Ascend the Nile,* is a muddy section of jungle in Rwanda's Nyungwe National Forest.† The water seeping from the earth then rolls downhill, becomes a stream, and finally a river that flows into the vast inland sea Speke located on August 3, 1858.

Others say that the source is a small bubbling spring in the mountains of Burundi, located in 1937 by Dr. Burkhardt Waldecker. The Kasumo, as this creek is known, is actually the source of a river known as the Ruvyironza, which, in turn, is a tributary of the 400-mile-long Kagera River that eventually flows into the lake Speke discovered.

Many a small jungle creek, in fact, can make a legitimate claim to being the one true source.

This bears repeating: there is no single source of the Nile River.

The truth is that thousands of remote jungle springs

*So named because they followed the legendary path of Herodotus, starting at the Mediterranean and becoming the first adventurers to travel backward up the river.
†A remote and nearly prehistoric mountainous rain forest that is home to 8 types of primate and 280 bird species—including rarities such as the Congo bay owl and African green broadbill, whose lineage dates back to such an early period in natural history that one guidebook refers to them as "living fossils."

eventually feed into the shimmering body of water on which Speke gazed that warm summer day in 1858.

So what had Speke discovered?

A historical asterisk.

Historical asterisks are misconceptions that get passed down through generations. In that time, two things happen: (1) the world at large comes to believe them as whole truth; and (2) history geeks study and debate them endlessly as a means of divining how we should record what really happened.

Christopher Columbus, for instance, is a historical asterisk. Elementary school textbooks say that he discovered America. There is a Columbus Day celebration on the second Monday each October each year to commemorate this achievement. However, every person who has visited or resided in North America since 1492 can rightfully claim that they got there before the great navigator. This is because Columbus never actually set foot on what is now US soil.*

That said, Columbus was the first European to build an enduring colony in the New World. We don't celebrate Columbus because he discovered the New World, but because he stayed.

---

*Columbus's explorations were confined to Cuba, the Bahamas, the Central American coast, South America, and the islands of the Caribbean.

This is no small feat. In fact, it changed the course of history. So rather than discredit Columbus entirely, as some would have it, better to give him the asterisk.

The same is true of Cook discovering Australia (Dutch navigator Willem Janszoon beat him by almost two centuries, but Cook still gets most of the credit); Robert Peary being first to reach the North Pole (every evidence points to him being off by as few as 5 miles or as many as dozens—and yes, he still gets the credit); and, as we are about to discover, Jack Speke and the source of the Nile.

John Hanning Speke's new body of water wasn't the ultimate source of the Nile. But it is the main outflow from its jungle beginning because a great and amazing waterfall floods out of its northern end. This mighty flow becomes something known as the White Nile, then merges with a second and completely different river known as the Blue Nile* near Khartoum, in what is now Sudan. At that point it is merely the Nile, which it remains until it rushes into the Mediterranean Sea, discharging 300 million cubic meters of water per day. So Speke did not actually discover the one true source, but the vast body of water through which the Nile flows during a very early portion of its 4,000-mile serpentine journey.

Thus, Speke's asterisk.

And it was that asterisk which led to the Nile duel.

---

*Born in the Ethiopian highlands, near Lake Tana, where it is originally known as the Abbai River.

2

Let's step back for a minute and imagine what must have been going through Speke's mind on that day. He is thirty-one years old. He has enjoyed a great deal of adventure in his life, but he hasn't achieved or discovered anything of note. He joined the army young, developed a reputation as a loner with a talent for hunting, enjoyed a weird sort of notoriety for surviving a battle with Somalia's penis-cutting people, and has spent the last year enduring the antics of a man prone to acts of infamy. His father is devoted to his heir and oldest son, his mother is so domineering that any man who can escape her craziness must do exactly that to avoid emasculation, he is widely considered to be illiterate, and British society thinks him a coward, thanks to Dick Burton's most recent book.

Speke has spent the day marching purposefully across yet another rolling African plain. Palm trees are everywhere. He is wearing those surreal stained glass eyeshades. He still has bits and pieces of beetle in his deaf ear. The air is humid and the sun bright. He has sweated through his clothes, which haven't been washed in weeks, so he doesn't smell fragrant in the best sense of the word.

Then something glimmers in the far distance.

For three long days he walks closer and closer to that body of water, until he finally stands on its shores. The surface is pale blue. He hears the quiet lap of the small waves and the cry of wheeling shore birds. A breeze caresses his face, carrying with it the enchanting smells of this previously uncharted inland sea.

Jack Speke is convinced of two things in an instant: (1) this is the source of the Nile. "I no longer had any doubt that the lake at my feet gave birth to that interesting river, the source of which has been the subject of so much speculation, and the object of so many explorers," he will later write. And: (2) he knows that his life is changed forever. Speke has just joined a select company of explorers who have found something once considered unattainable. Others lucky enough to experience such a moment of superlative discovery describe it with an almost sexual euphoria. "To solve a problem which has long resisted the skill and persistence of others is an irresistible magnet in every sphere of human activity" is how Sir John Hunt, leader of the successful 1953 Everest expedition, breathlessly described that achievement. "There is no height, no depth, that the spirit of man cannot attain."

Speke chose to name this grand body of water Victoria, an over-the-top gesture in honor of Britain's queen. One does not name puddles in the jungle after monarchs. One names lakes wider than the English Channel after a royal with twenty years on the throne—and forty-three years to go. It helps that the well-heeled Speke most likely remembered that the anniversary of Victoria's coronation was just a month away.

The grandiosity continued. Just in case anyone might forget that Speke's discovery was the biggest lake he had

ever seen,* he added the redundancy of the word Nyanza.
This was a Bantu word meaning a large body of water, or sea.
Hence, Victoria Nyanza. Never mind that the Arabs and the
indigenous tribes of central Africa had already given it several
names, among them Ukewere, Sango, Lolwe, and Nalubaale.
From this day forward, the lake would bear the name given
it by Speke—as it still does today, despite ongoing efforts to
change it.

Victoria Nyanza's enormity was an answered prayer. No
minor body of water could possibly give birth to the Nile.
Once he had firmly established this in his head, Speke immediately began discrediting Burton's theories. The animosity
between the two men had been building for a year. Now, as it
came to a head, Speke confidently began expressing his own
opinions: "This is a far more extensive lake than Tanganyika, so
broad that you could not see across it, and so long that no one
knew its length."

The discovery of what would come to be known as Lake
Victoria marked the moment when the Burton and Speke relationship began the adversarial path that it would follow for
the next six years. And while Speke was quite sure that Lake
Victoria was the outflow of the Nile, Burton still had a very
legitimate reason for arguing in favor of Tanganyika.

---

*And second largest in the world. North America's Lake Superior is the
biggest.

The streams flowing into Victoria from the southwest (whether the mountains of modern Burundi or those of Rwanda) are roughly halfway between Lake Victoria and Lake Tanganyika. Since almost nothing was known about that area, and because Burton and Speke hadn't bothered looking at the Rusizi with their own eyes to discover whether it flowed out of Tanganyika, there was a very real possibility that an undiscovered river connected them all. This, of course, would mean that Burton was correct. He would later argue that Speke might have found *a* source, but not *the* source.

This would form the basic premise of the Nile duel.

If only Burton and Speke had followed their RGS orders and explored the lands between Tanganyika and Victoria, they would have discovered an enormous watershed in the mountainous jungles. This would have shown them conclusively that something now known as the "Albertine Rift" connects a different chain of lakes* and has no connection to the Nile, which is fed from a separate watershed.

None of the rancor or bile between the two explorers that would soon consume Victorian London would have existed— if only they had been more thorough in completing their assignment.

Just as Burton became the first European to set eyes on Tanganyika, so Speke now had Victoria. When it was time to turn around and return to Kazeh, Speke professed to being

*North to south: Albert, Edward, Kivu, Tanganyika, Rukwa, Malawi.

so in love with his splendid discovery that he felt "as much grieved as any mother would be at losing her firstborn, and planned to do everything in my power to visit the lake again."

3

Use of the possessive pronoun was clearly a marker of Speke's growing independence, the fifth trait of the explorers. Some explorers preferred solitude on their journeys, and others companionship. No matter what their preference, a deep desire for taking charge of destiny attended their approach to life. Their thoughts and words demonstrated a deep desire to chart their own course, even—perhaps especially—when others thought them foolish. Their personal satisfaction could only be attained by pressing onward toward a goal, never doubting in their ability to achieve it.

The term "independence" is an oxymoron of sorts, with some aspects of society viewing such behavior as rebellion and others as a virtue. Independence is neither. It is simply the ability to make decisions for oneself, take responsibility for the consequences, and ensure that these decisions are socially and morally appropriate—all the while pushing oneself to manifest their highest potential.

The key word in each of those three criteria is "decisions." A person cannot be independent if they are not decisive.

But this is just the starting point. Cognitive psychologist Herman Witkin found that people who lack independence also tend to lack self-direction, are happiest when taking orders from others, tend to be deeply fearful of disapproval, conform compulsively, and largely spend their entire lives as what can only politely be described as spectators.

Independent individuals, on the other hand, constantly pursue their highest potential. They are inner-directed, following their hearts and goals, not defining themselves by others to be happy. Their self-worth does not come through society's expectations, but through following their inner quests to their ultimate conclusion. The need for approval that presents itself in the nonindependent ("I must be *liked* by you to be happy") is either minimal or nonexistent. The truly independent have an ability to create structure in the middle of chaos, have the sorts of hyperfocused memory that allows them to categorize and recall data, and are almost devoid of envy ("I must be *like* you to be happy") because it is the antithesis of what it means to think and feel for oneself.

They are also, to a large extent, introverts. Researchers still struggle to define the difference between an introvert and an extrovert, but the normal litmus test is one simple question: how do you recharge your emotional batteries? Extroverts are energized by being around people—through discussion, engagement, and connection. Introverts, on the other hand, top off their emotional fuel tanks by being alone. They find time spent with other people to be draining. It is for this reason that introverts don't do well in group brainstorming sessions, corporate meetings, and team-oriented activities.

However, they are often the creators and thinkers of the world—imagine Picasso, Da Vinci, and pretty much every writer who has ever lived. This is because they thrive on spending hours alone, getting lost in their work, and not requiring other human interaction to complete their task.

Shackleton, Columbus, Cook, Stanley, Livingstone, Speke, and even the gregarious Burton were introverts. Introversion was as synonymous with exploration as risk. Explorers were capable of spending—quite happily, I might add—years away from traditional society. When *Apollo 11* traveled to the moon in 1969, the outbound journey lasted just three days, three hours, and forty-nine minutes. When an Air France Concorde set the around-the-world speed record in 1996, it took just thirty-one hours and twenty-eight minutes to travel from New York to New York at twice the speed of sound.* Even now, traveling from Dar es Salaam to Kigoma aboard the plodding and dilapidated Tanzanian National Railway takes just twenty-four hours. And it's not even worth mentioning that the invention of the satellite phone made it possible to communicate with anyone, anywhere, instantly.

Compare all that with explorers, who left friends, wives, children, and essentially their entire lives for years at a time.

---

*I was lucky enough to be a passenger on that flight. There were refueling stops in Toulouse, Dubai, Bangkok, Guam, Honolulu, and Acapulco. A seven-course meal was served for each leg of the flight, complete with wine pairings. The chant from the other passengers as we finally landed once again in New York was "one more lap."

There was little communication with the outside world. Those letters from home that somehow found them in the middle of nowhere were typically written a year or more earlier. Travel mostly took place on foot. A good day was considered to be anything more than 15 miles. There were endless periods of utter boredom—without books, music, television, iPads, iPods, video games, or a laptop to serve as distractions. And yet this bent toward introversion made it all possible, because many explorers lived most happily inside their heads. Many, in fact, were social clods, ill at ease in high society, and freakishly out of step with the normal world. But put them in a foreign land, make them walk through a burning desert, or let them grasp the wheel of a ship battling 100-foot seas, and these people thrived.

There's one other aspect of introversion that is very germane to the story of Burton and Speke. As social scientist Susan Cain has written, introverts tend to be very thin-skinned. They feel things more deeply and passionately than extroverts. They hold on tightly to these emotions, nursing grudges and plotting revenge as they live through higher highs and lower lows. The Nile duel may have had its roots in Africa, but its abiding jealousy, rage, and entitlement were nurtured by the introversion of Burton and Speke.

4

There's little they could have done about it. Introversion is an inherited personality trait, hard-wired into our brains at birth. An estimated one half to three fourths of the world's population lack the introvert's fondness for hyperfocus and long hours of alone time. Happily, that does not exclude extroverts from developing the independence trait. It starts by being self-directed. This involves setting personal goals, and then looking inward for ways to achieve them. This is the opposite of asking permission, or leaning on mentors or life coaches or any of a number of self-styled gurus to lead the way. This is because true independence is a constant striving to know oneself better, and to constantly reset personal expectations and ambitions in an effort to achieve your highest potential. Manipulation by other individuals detracts from this process.

This quest for self-knowledge ultimately leads to an examination of character as the motivations about why a goal is all-important make themselves known. So the process of becoming truly independent is also a long-term investment in becoming a better person. Artifice is stripped away, ethics and morals become important, and an inclination toward purity in thought and behavior become one with the courage of deeply held convictions.

This is partly because that constant examination of character is as much a part of achieving an individual's highest potential as any outlandish goal one might pursue; it is also partly because those striving for independence soon learn a hard truth: they are being watched.

Independent persons, by definition, are individuals set apart. They make people uncomfortable. Independent people remind us when we are not pushing our own limits and living our lives to the fullest. The independent person's path and behavior will constantly be scrutinized, and often mocked, by those who would prefer to go along with the crowd. High moral and ethical character becomes vital armor to silencing these critics; and even those virtuous traits are often mocked by those who don't strive toward them.

Success, of course, in all aspects of life, is an even more powerful protection.

The great irony is that truly independent people don't care. They are set apart from society, following their own compass, marching to the beat of a drum that only they can hear. Explorers were fond of reminding themselves that their biggest foe wasn't a hostile landscape or the raging sea, but the six inches between their ears. Forcing themselves to silence self-doubts, no matter how dire the predicament, gave them the strength to carry on. "We should refuse none of the thousand and one joys that the mountain offers us at every turn. We should brush nothing aside, set no restrictions. We should experience hunger and thirst, be able to go fast, but also know how to go slowly and contemplate. Variety is the spice of life," wrote one French climber.

Left unsaid is that "variety" means the same as "danger."

How else to explain the ability to enjoy deprivation and suffering while dangling from a thin rope upon a rock face some thousand feet off the ground?

Small wonder that history's great explorers are models of independence.

But again, that trait was not hard-wired into their DNA. It is learned through the process of attempting any great undertaking: curiosity, hope, courage, and passion must all take place before true independence is achieved.

5

By the dawn of the twentieth century, worldwide exploration had come to a standstill. The major continents had not only been charted, but were riven with infrastructure. The term "civilized" was used more and more to describe corners of the globe that had once been just blank spots on the map. With nowhere else to go, the path of exploration, for a time, magically turned upward, thanks to the discovery of flight. Since the earliest days of exploration, travelers had either sailed a ship, walked on foot, ridden an animal, or paddled a small boat. Orville and Wilbur Wright's invention of the airplane offered explorers a whole new means of travel. The discovery of the skies, with their invisible currents and turbulence and countless methods of thwarting the act of flight, added a completely different dimension to exploration. Each takeoff promised a test of skill, an education, and a journey of discovery.

Everyone from Roald Amundsen to Winston Churchill soon learned to fly. It became possible to explore the Amazon or Africa or the Rockies from the air, looking down for new perspectives, or landing in some far-off spot, thus saving months and even years of travel time (and the encounters with disease and warfare that ultimately accompanied those journeys).

But it was the great long-distance journeys that most captured the public's imagination: Lindbergh's flight across the Atlantic, Wiley Post flying around the world, Amelia Earhart's legendary journeys, and ultimately the Apollo lunar missions. These and other flights marked the aviation epoch as an earth-changing age of exploration.

Aviation became synonymous with independence. From its earliest days, exploration of the air demanded that pilots be self-reliant in ways that most others would deem either irresponsible or downright mad—but that those flying the aircraft realized was all part of surpassing their mental, physical, and emotional limits. Pilots even came up with a term for this behavior: "pushing the edge of the envelope." In spirit it means the same as the more mundane "thinking outside the box," but takes on a much more powerful meaning when flaring the afterburner nozzle to launch off a ship's deck or punch through the sound barrier.

Very often this mental toughness took on a tone of humility. World War II British fighter pilot Richard Hillary wrote of challenging his resolve and skills by flying his Spitfire under a bridge so low to the water, and so tight between supports that he could only make it with inches to spare—if he made it at all. Hillary mentioned this idea to Peter Pease, a fellow Spitfire pilot. Pease's thoughtful reply is a classic: "Richard, from now on a lot of people are going to fly under that bridge. From a flying point of view it proves nothing; it's extremely stupid. From a personal point of view it can only be of value if you don't tell anybody about it."

Hillary recorded the moment in his journal: "Yet I knew I would fly under it. I had to for my own satisfaction, just as many years before I had to stand on a twenty-five-foot board above a swimming pool until I had dived off."

Hillary made it—barely. He was later shot down and killed in World War II. We only know of the achievement through the posthumous publication of his journals.

Or take the case of aviation pioneer Amy Johnson. In the 1920s, when flying was the domain of men, Johnson ignored naysayers and doubters to break into the boys' club. The daughter of a fish merchant from northern England, she was enchanted by the barnstorming pilots who passed through their small village. In 1928, at age twenty-five, she quit her job as a typist and enrolled at a small flight school, performing secretarial work in exchange for tuition.

Johnson was by no means a natural pilot. Her instructors told her she had no aptitude for flying. She got hopelessly lost on her first solo flight. But Johnson ignored them, instead focusing on learning aircraft maintenance in addition to earning her wings. By December 1929 she had become the first female aircraft mechanic in England.

This might have been enough for someone less head-strong, but Johnson had a passion for flight. In May 1930, she bought a secondhand Gipsy Moth biplane, painted it green, gave it the moniker *Jason*, and then abruptly took off from Croydon Airfield. She had accumulated only seventy-five hours of flight time, her longest flight to date was just 147 miles long, and she knew little about navigation, and yet John-son's ambitious goal was nothing less than to fly from London, England, to Sydney, Australia. "The prospect did not frighten me, because I was so appallingly ignorant that I never realized in the least what I had taken on," she later wrote.

It took Johnson two days to reach Istanbul. From there she set off alone over the deserts of Iraq and Iran, where she landed in a sandstorm. After using her suitcase as a wheel chock, she covered the entire aircraft in canvas and waited out the storm with a revolver in one hand, just in case of attack. The next day she reached Baghdad. The day after that, Oman.

Johnson landed in Karachi, Pakistan, the next day. All told, she had been traveling for just less than a week. It dawned on her that she might actually break the London-to-Sydney speed record of fifteen days, set just two years earlier. At the pace she was flying, Johnson estimated she would break that mark by almost three days.

Setting out from Karachi, Johnson ran out of fuel over the town of Jhansi. She glided to a landing on the parade ground of a British military post, scattering the marching soldiers. From there it was on to Calcutta and Rangoon, where she flew into the teeth of a monsoon and nearly crashed. Flying between Bangkok and Singapore, she got hopelessly lost and fell behind the record pace. However, news of her journey was following Johnson. As she banked to land in Singapore, she was astounded to see thousands of the colony's residents awaiting her arrival.

Two days later, Johnson landed *Jason* in Sydney. Telegrams from the king and queen of England, Charles Lindbergh, and other dignitaries soon arrived. By the time she sailed home to England, Johnson was known far and wide as the "Aeroplane Girl."

Amy Johnson went on to break numerous distance records. Amelia Earhart became a close friend, and Johnson was devastated when her American counterpart disappeared. When World War II broke out, Johnson's application to join the Royal Air Force was rejected. Instead, she was put to work ferrying new aircraft from their factories to various squadrons. She died on January 5, 1941, flying the mail, when her plane crashed into the Thames. Her body was never retrieved.

6

Even though Johnson and Hillary both died while flying, and their actual "discoveries" appear minimal on the surface, their experiences contributed to the continuum of acquired avia-

tion knowledge that eventually landed men on the moon—
and got them home again*—thus concluding a broader arc of
venturing out into the unknown that began with Brendan.

But if aviation often symbolizes the spirit of independence, it's worth noting that one epoch of exploration history
twines the independence of the explorers with the character
of the budding nation itself. In fact, it can be argued that there
would be no United States of America without a citizenry
begun by exploration, expanded by exploration, and almost
completely defined by an independent spirit that demanded
exploration.

There has never been another nation in history that literally encouraged its people to gather their belongings, leave

---

*Space, as *Star Trek*'s Captain Kirk so blithely put it, is the final frontier.
Since the dawn of time, man has gazed up at the nighttime sky and
dreamed of touching the moon. On July 21, 1969, less than three decades after the first crude rockets were launched against England during
the Battle of Britain, man used that same transportation to set foot on
the lunar surface. Neil Armstrong called it his "giant leap for mankind,"
though he said it somewhat tongue in cheek. Armstrong was afraid the
moon's soil might be thin silt, into which he would sink up to his knees.
As he made the leap, he held on to the Apollo spacecraft's lunar module,
just to make sure he didn't fall over.

Space not only ended the era of exploration, it also ended the
public's fascination with explorers. I have written before that explorers
were the rock stars of their eras, individuals so famous they were often
mobbed in the streets. As evidenced by the hero worship directed at
the original seven Mercury astronauts, not much changed during the
buildup to space travel. In terms of exploration, however, they were the
last rock stars.

their homes and families, and then tramp thousands of miles across a hostile and rugged wilderness to find a better life. What happened in America between 1804 (the journey of Lewis and Clark that opened the American frontier) and 1893 (when it was formally decreed that the frontier was closed) is unparalleled. It would be as if a large percentage of Great Britain's population up and walked to Russia, there to take over the country, build a new life, and never return home.*

The exploration of North America began in earnest with Columbus's discovery of the New World in 1492, and continued until that declaration that the frontier was closed more than four hundred years later. This is one of the most well-known but misunderstood periods in the history of exploration. It is frequently viewed in nationalist terms (the exploration of the US, say, as opposed to the entire continent. Charting Canada was no less arduous nor epic), but it's important to note that the works of dozens of explorers complemented one another, leading to a thorough understanding of North America—Boone, Crockett, Lewis and Clark, Frémont, and many more. Even Teddy Roosevelt, whose "man in the arena" speech opens

---

*Two thoughts on this: to truly reenact America's westward expansion using this scenario, these transient Britons would be allowed to settle and build a home at any point along this journey—displacing by force anyone who already lived there. And it can be argued that such a mythical mass migration is taking place in reverse during the early parts of the twenty-first century. Previous residents of the USSR have flooded into London in a way that would have seemed farcical during the Soviet years.

this chapter as a verbal embodiment of independence, makes an appearance—albeit in South America. The former president and rookie explorer's dreadful 1913–14 journey down Brazil's Rio da Duvida—River of Doubt—traced the path of the last great uncharted river in the Americas. Roosevelt's account of the journey was so farfetched that he was forced to publicly defend his findings, which he did successfully.

The same would ultimately be true of Burton and Speke.

On August 25, less than three weeks after beginning his return journey, Speke arrived at Burton's temporary residence in Kazeh "in a state of high spirits and gratification." It was morning. Burton was about to eat breakfast. Speke described the enormity of Victoria Nyanza, but for the majority of the meal danced around the subject of it being The Source. However, at the end of breakfast Speke put forth his theory. He also proposed that they march back to the lake and sail from one side to the other to find the Nile's headwaters. "We had scarcely breakfasted," Burton wrote, "before he announced to me the startling fact that he had discovered the sources of the Nile. The fortunate discoverer's conviction was strong, but his reasoning was weak."

To say that Speke's announcement did not go over well is a gross understatement. Burton "expressed regret that he did not accompany me," Speke later wrote. "I felt certain in my mind I had discovered the source of the Nile. This he naturally objected to, even after hearing all my reasons for saying so."

Even as Burton struggled to reconcile whether Speke

might be right, he was also coming to the realization that he would be upstaged if this was the case. The entire journey would be viewed through the prism of Speke's heroic solo journey to Victoria Nyanza. Never before had Burton been seen as anything less than the daring sparkplug of adventure. He had fully expected to receive the same sort of welcome upon arriving in London with news about Lake Tanganyika. Now that was not to be. Burton began looking for ways to discredit his subordinate. "Although I had pursued my journey under great provocations from time to time, I never realized what an injury I had done the expedition publicly, as well as myself, by not traveling alone, or with Arab companions, or at least with a less crooked-minded, cantankerous English," Burton later wrote.

By the time they began their journey back to Zanzibar one month later, Burton and Speke were barely talking to one another. And when they did, the topic of the two lakes and the Nile River was not discussed.

The trek seemed interminable. Speke made the divide worse when he contracted an unspecified nerve disease that caused burning sensations in his torso, vicious nightmares, muscle spasms, and rage-filled delirium. In one of these half-crazed moments, Speke railed about the many ways that Burton had publicly defamed his character. Burton perceived this as an attempt by Speke to take over as expedition leader, rather than accepting that his companion was half out of his mind.

On March 4, 1859, five long months after leaving Kazeh, Burton and Speke reached Zanzibar. From there they caught a clipper ship named *Dragon of Salem* for Aden. On April 19, the HMS *Furious* arrived in port to refill her coal supplies. From there, she would travel up the Red Sea to the Suez.* Speke accepted an offer to continue his journey home aboard *Furious*. Burton did not, explaining that he was in no hurry to return.

It was a mistake he would regret for the rest of his life.

7

So it was that Jack Speke reached London and the Royal Geographical Society on May 8. Dick Burton arrived on May 21, to what could only have been a most horrific homecoming. Within a day of his return, Speke had been invited to the monthly meeting of the RGS. At the time, their headquarters were at Whitehall Place, mere blocks from Speke's hotel in Piccadilly. Thanks to the occasional letter from Africa, the

---

*At that time, travel through the Suez desert involved a 100-mile overland crossing from the Red Sea to the Mediterranean. Construction of the Suez Canal began on April 25, 1859, which is precisely when Speke passed through the region. It's worth noting that the British government adamantly opposed this French building project, because it threatened their control of high seas. The Suez Canal opened in 1869, and is notable for not having any locks. The Panama Canal (which was first undertaken in the 1880s by Ferdinand de Lesseps, the same man who built the Suez Canal) has six.

RGS was well aware that Speke had been responsible for the expedition's cartography, owing to his ingenious use of lunar sighting to establish longitude.

On May 9, Speke met privately with Sir Roderick Murchison and showed his map of Victoria Nyanza. Not only did Murchison eagerly endorse Speke's view that this was the source, he immediately demanded that Speke return to Africa and lead another expedition to the lake—this time with Speke himself in command. Speke's enthusiastic acceptance, despite the fact that he had just returned from three years of living hell, immediately rekindled the curiosity that began the exploration cycle all over again.

By the time Burton's ship was docking at Southampton, his exploration career had already been eclipsed. "I reached London on May 21st," he lamented, "and found that everything had been done for, or rather against, me."

There was no more glory to be had, for that was all being lavished upon Speke. The man six years Burton's junior was not only the toast of the exploration world, but all of London as well.

Burton's physical appearance didn't help matters a bit. He was, in the words of his beloved Isabel, "a mere skeleton, with brown yellow skin hanging in bags, his eyes protruding, and his lips drawn away from his teeth."

Small wonder that the RGS gave scant consideration to a proposal by Burton that he lead this second expedition into Africa.

Over the next year, the divide between Burton and Speke grew until there was no hope for reconciliation. Petty squabbles about the publication of Speke's journals and the settling of the expedition's finances entered into the equation. By April 1860 it was clear that the two men would never again be on speaking terms. This didn't stop Speke from making one last effort to bridge the divide. "My dear Burton," he wrote in a letter on the eve of his return to Africa, "I cannot leave England addressing you so coldly as you have hitherto been responding."

Burton scribbled this reply in pencil on the letter's margins: "Any other tone would be distasteful to me."

On April 27, 1860, Jack Speke boarded the British warship HMS *Forte* in Southampton, bound for Zanzibar. His troubles with Burton were set aside, at least for the next few years, replaced by the enormity of what he was about to attempt. The plan was for Speke and his new traveling companion James Grant to literally follow the Nile from source to sea; from Victoria Nyanza to the Mediterranean. It would be the longest and most ambitious expedition in the history of African exploration.

And, much to Dick Burton's chagrin, it would be a rousing success.

8

It is somewhat mind-boggling to step back and analyze the outrageousness of Speke's plan. The distance was almost 5,000 miles. He would once again endure the malaria and other diseases that had nearly killed him. Those dangers he had already experienced would be revisited, with a host of new life-threatening encounters sure to join that list as he made his way into the unknown regions of the Nile basin, including having to make his way across the legendary Sudd. The achievement had never been accomplished in the entire history of man, and on the surface was downright impossible.

However, if Speke ever drew up what would today be called a bucket list, walking the length of the Nile River would have been at the very top. Having seen its source, he now needed to revel in the rest of it. His life would not be complete until he did so. Speke's name was now synonymous with the Nile, and his emotional connection to the river surpassed even that to the Victoria Nyanza.

What is most remarkable is not that Speke undertook that journey, nor that he did so within a year of his horrendous adventure with Burton. What stands out most vividly is that Speke never outwardly expressed a moment of fear. There is nothing in his journals that talks to the darkness or doubt that would course through most men.

But surely it existed, just as it exists in all of us before a great challenge. Perhaps he woke up in the middle of the night, thinking of the tribe that sliced off the genitals and arms of the French lieutenant Maizan while he was still alive. Maybe, standing alone on the deck of *Forte* as Southampton receded into the distance, he wondered if he would ever again see England. If he thought of death, did Speke wonder if his body might receive a proper burial? Or would it be left to rot on an anonymous African plain, the flesh and muscles ripped from his bones by lions and carrion birds before hyenas finished the job by eating the bones themselves and digesting them in those special stomach acids of theirs, ensuring that there would be nothing left to find of John Hanning Speke should someone ever come looking.

That certainly wasn't the sort of thing the average Englishman ever had to ponder. So such a thought would be quite rational.

It's not that Speke didn't experience fear. He wouldn't be human if the occasional moment of doubt or terror didn't flood his brain. It's just that he was quietly and incredibly self-disciplined about his behavior when such moments arose.

SELF-DISCIPLINE

Perhaps it is this conquest, conquest of one's self through survival of such an ordeal, that brings a man back to frontiers again and again. It may be a storm, the arctic cold, or the desert heat. It may be a frontier of the spirit or of the mind. By testing himself beyond endurance man learns to know himself. He endures and grows. Each generation passes the limits defined by its elders: the passage of the oceans, the reaching of the poles, flight, the four-minute mile, the theory of relativity, atomic fission. In a small way, the conquest of a great peak is such a frontier.

—Charles Houston, after summiting K2,
the world's second-highest peak

1

Speke needed to find the waterfall. It was imperative he locate that great northward outflow from Victoria Nyanza that would prove its connection to the Nile. That's why he had come back to Africa—that, and the never before accomplished challenge of following the Nile all the way to Cairo.

The Speke-Grant expedition was launched in Bagamoyo on October 2, 1860, with Speke, his friend and fellow army veteran James Grant, the caravan leader and guide Sidi Mubarak Bombay, and the same long line of porters whom Speke and Burton once employed. And while their journey actually set forth from that Indian Ocean beach with the gentle rollers, the true jumping-off point would not come until they reached the shores of Victoria Nyanza. In between lay 1,000 miles of the same trials and hardships that Speke had endured with Burton; the same diseases, bugs, snakes, predators, hostile tribes, heat, mud, abject terror, and boredom.

Grant and Speke soon fell hopelessly behind schedule. They were cut off entirely from any sort of rescue as they penetrated deeper into the continent, and, as they finally drew nearer to Victoria Nyanza, heard rumors that a great African ruler had just sacrificed more than four hundred people to celebrate their arrival. Once the great lake was almost within their sights, that informal network of spoken-word messengers known as the bush telegraph brought more gossip of a king who refused to allow travelers to travel northward out of his country—precisely the direction Speke and Grant were headed.

And yet Speke and Grant remained completely undeterred. Some code, some inner drive, some sense of purpose, would not let Jack Speke and James Grant turn back.

They needed to find that waterfall.

2

Self-discipline is all about action. It can be defined as emotional control, physical control, and behavioral control, and on this first journey as expedition leader, Speke offered a steely demonstration of all three. It helped that he got along well with his new travel partner, which was a welcome change to the personnel roster after the daily upheaval with Burton. Speke had become quite familiar with Africa during his previous journeys, and proved himself both fearless and canny when dealing with the Arabs and local tribes. He preferred to broker peace rather than using his considerable shooting skills to wage war or inflict terror. He overcame the daily fear and uncertainty that existed side by side within a journey beyond the realms of a surefire support or resupply network. And he behaved throughout like the most stellar example of an English gentleman, comporting himself with such grace and ease that it was as if he felt he would have to answer to some nameless etiquette authority upon his return to London should he become a boor.

The most striking aspect of all this was that Speke's knowledge of Africa was limited to the small regions through which he and Burton had traveled. He knew nothing about the unknown lakes and peoples between Victoria Nyanza and Cairo. Yet throughout the journey, Speke was so confident in his ability to complete his mission that it was as if he knew far more.

This is known as self-efficacy.

Self-efficacy is simply a belief in one's own competence. "Efficacy" comes from the Latin *efficacia*, a derivation of *efficere*, which means "to accomplish." The seminal psychologist Albert Bandura, whose landmark 1977 paper "Self-Efficacy: Toward a Unifying Theory of Behavioral Change" thrust accomplishment to the forefront of psychological research, describes it as "the belief in one's capabilities to organize and execute the courses of action required to manage prospective situations."

In other words, the ability to get the job done.

As Bandura has noted, "Self-belief does not necessarily ensure success, but self-disbelief assuredly spawns failure."

But belief alone cannot complete a task, which is where the secondary component of self-discipline comes into play. This is known as self-mastery, and is defined as the harnessing of personal strengths and weaknesses to complete a goal. Together, self-efficacy and self-mastery form the two halves of self-discipline. If self-efficacy can be characterized as the determination to see a mission through to its completion, self-mastery is the necessary character modification needed to make that dream a reality.

This is a highly personal process. We are all different in the skills that we possess and the way in which we rein them in to complete our unique adventures. Sometimes this behavior modification is something as simple as a list of new dos and don'ts. The most common example is a weight loss program, with its requirements for more sleep, better hydration, less alcohol, less red meat, more vegetables, and a more logical and minimal caloric intake. Sounds simple, but we all know that is not the case. Habits and routines are hard to reroute, and the decision to consciously choose self-denial over comfort often needs to be repeated again and again and again.

There are other times when the behavior modification is a decision to control emotions, particularly when a journey becomes so grueling as to appear hopeless. For instance, one of the great caricatures of the Victorian explorer was that British ideal of portraying "a stiff upper lip" in times of danger. It implied a cool nonchalance, a steely backbone, and a sense of propriety. This was how Speke behaved.

It has been written that modern aircraft pilots owe their preternaturally calm in-flight demeanor to Chuck Yeager, the first man to break the sound barrier. Before him, radio chatter might be laced with whooping, hollering, and a general all-around display of emotions. But whether punching through Mach I or engaging in a World War II dogfight, the laconic Yeager maintained a calm monotone, as if such adventures were something he was observing with detachment. This cool delivery caught on, which was probably a good thing for commercial aviation. Not many of us would feel comfortable in a pressurized metal tube flown by a man screaming into the public address system about the jet stream and turbofan engines and anvil-headed clouds taking control of his aircraft. We want to know that the pilot is in charge, which is exactly what Yeager conveyed. He must have known some sense of panic or fear, but he never showed it. This is emotional self-discipline.

Speke was the Victorian Yeager. He wandered through the wilderness with the same casual intensity one might apply to a Sunday walk through Hyde Park. He became the Victorian model of how an explorer should behave. Interestingly, Speke and Yeager both model the revolving door of self-efficacy and self-mastery. According to Bandura, the ability to get the job done is enhanced through mastery experiences and the kudos that come with success. So for every act of discipline and self-control that eventually got an explorer through a journey, their confidence grew. And the next time they were challenged to do something that seemed impossible, not only did they find a way to accomplish that task, but they very often considered themselves to be the only individual capable of doing so. Some might have seen this as arrogance. In fact, this attitude was vital to the completion of their mission.

As Bandura has noted: "People with high assurance in

their capabilities approach difficult tasks as challenges to be mastered rather than as threats to be avoided."

3

Why, specifically, is self-discipline an important practice?

Perhaps the Catholic priest Basil William Maturin, who went down when the *Lusitania* was torpedoed by the Germans in World War I, has the answer. "We do not endure [self-discipline] merely for its own sake, but for what lies beyond it. And we bear those acts of self-denial and self-restraint because we feel and know full well that through such acts alone can we regain the mastery over all our misused powers and learn to use them with a vigor and a joy such as we have never known before," he wrote one year before drowning.

These words closely resemble those of the Apostle Paul: "For we rejoice in our sufferings, because suffering produces perseverance; perseverance produces character; and, character produces hope. And hope does not disappoint us."

What happens when we don't endure the hardship of self-discipline? In modern life, those who spend too much, drink too much, inhale forbidden substances, and cheat on their spouses are immediately cast out as examples of people lacking self-discipline. But no one mentions what, specifically, constitutes the inverse. Self-discipline is not just the tool that saves us from throwing our lives upon the Viking bonfire of self-dissipation. It is also the path to a richer and fuller life. To walk down that path is to begin a journey of personal exploration no less daunting than any foray into Africa. We learn things about ourselves when we take the challenge to rein in our emotions, our impulses, and our pride.

Father Maturin speaks of that "joy such as we have never known before," while explorers like the Frenchman Gaston Rebuffat speaks of "A power, a balance and reserve that normally lie dormant" that accompanies such acts of will.

The basis of all exploration was relentless pursuit of a dream. Regardless of calamity, setback, suffering, and woe, the final result was all that mattered. Giving up, no matter how valid the excuses, was considered an act of failure. So it was that explorers pushed themselves to their mental, physical, and emotional limits to achieve their mission.

Rather than being weakened by these ordeals, the explorers became stronger. Reaching their goal—finding the source of the Nile, reaching the South Pole, and so many others—was in many ways less satisfying than the sublime daily ritual of disciplining their minds and bodies to do the hard work necessary to complete their task. The polar explorer Martin Lindsay described it simply as "the pleasure one so surprisingly gets from trying to do something that is difficult."

The problem with self-discipline is its extremist reputation. One imagines US Marine Corps drill instructors, flagellant priests, or the obsessive-compulsives who all too often inhabit the world of Ironman Triathlon. In fact, self-discipline just as often defines the daily routine of the successful artist or snowboarder. There is the perhaps apocryphal story of Ernest Hemingway making a personal promise not to drink a drop of alcohol until finishing his writing day. As the legend goes, Hemingway often remained true to that ideal by beginning his writing day very early in the morning, just so he could settle into his seat at the bar by noon.*

In its own convoluted way, that is self-discipline. *A Farewell to Arms*, *For Whom the Bell Tolls*, and *The Old Man and the Sea* don't happen without that well-intentioned but ultimately absurd daily promise.

To be self-disciplined is not to be perfect. It is to be striving toward a personal ideal that is different for each and every one of us. "In reading the lives of great men," Harry Truman once said, "I found that the first victory they won was over themselves. Self-discipline with all of them came first."

Whether done quickly or slowly, the process of attaining Speke-like self-discipline practiced by explorers followed five simple characteristics: (1) self-awareness: knowing one-

---

*Hemingway once famously said that he drank "to make other people more interesting." The *Times* of London reported on December 14, 2013, that researchers in Finland and Britain discovered that many intelligent people do the very same thing. The London School of Economics collected data from 17,000 people born in Britain in 1958 as part of the National Childhood Development Study. Their findings show a correlation between an elevated IQ and the tendency to enjoy an adult beverage. The *Times* went on to suggest that those with higher IQs needed a drink "after a hard day dealing with stupid nondrinkers"—which puts its own spin on Hemingway's quote.

self well enough to address weaknesses; (2) confrontation: a resolution to deal with a problem head-on; (3) commitment: adopt whatever new discipline is vital to complete a mission and perform it each day; (4) acceptance: stay positive, and realize that negative events are daily facts of life; and (5) respect: be good to yourself; self-discipline is not easy.

Speke was robbed, imprisoned, caught in a war, tempted with the gift of a teenage girl for a bed partner, forced to play the role of doctor to an African queen, ambushed by hostile tribes, endured porters who deserted and stole precious supplies, forced to witness a child being boiled alive, lost Grant for a time to severe illness, and suffered his own host of inevitable African sicknesses.

If anything, the hardships faced by Speke and Grant were far greater than those endured during the Speke and Burton Expedition. Speke and Grant—a Scot who had lost a thumb and forefinger while besieged during the Indian Mutiny of 1857–58—witnessed the execution of a man whose genitals were set on fire before he was ultimately stabbed; endured sickness leading to paralysis; was imprisoned by a hostile chieftain; knew the wrenching pain of a swollen spleen; and spent Christmas of 1861 with a king who force-fed his daughters beef drippings and fresh milk until they were obese, as a way of proving his great wealth and prosperity.

Speke and Grant endured malarias, diarrheas, joint pains, infections, and neuromuscular paralysis. There were countless delays and setbacks. There were bouts of loneliness, exhaustion, and adversity. There was, all around them, a vast and unforgiving landscape that had crushed the soul of many a traveler—and killed many, many more. It was a continent so hostile, so vast, and so treacherous that even the Africans Speke encountered along the journey were afraid to venture beyond their tribal boundaries.

But Speke led Grant through these trials by practicing a steely sort of self-discipline, comprised of habits and inner strength that allowed him to rise above his surroundings. Speke wrote with great detail in his journal each day, finding solace in the routine, knowing that someday these words being cobbled together in his tent, or before a campfire, would be part of his legacy, for they were his proof of his accomplishment. Speke kept his temper, even when African chiefs delayed his travels for their own amusement. He stayed on task, never losing sight of his goal of finding that all-important waterfall. And, most of all, Jack Speke pressed on toward his ultimate goal of becoming the first man in history to trace the Nile from one end to the other. He never ceased to tap into the inner power, personal balance, and normally dormant reserve of self-discipline that would see him through to his goal—especially in times of fear and self-doubt. In time, the word "mindfulness" would be applied to this mode of behavior. But Speke was hardly Zen. He simply thought of self-discipline as a means of getting the job done.

It was self-efficacy that led Speke to boldly propose that the RGS send him back into Africa to verify the source, thinking himself the best man for the job. In all of the world, Speke was convinced that he alone could accomplish this monumental task.

But once he got into Africa, that veneer of confidence was replaced by the mastery skills needed to get up each morning and put one foot in front of the other, even on days when turning around and fleeing back to London was quite obviously the wise thing to do.

Thus, Speke ultimately found his waterfall.

4

The sight disappointed him.

The wellsprings of the Nile thundered out of Lake Victoria in a broad line some 400 feet across, by Speke's estimation. "The roar of the waters, the thousands of passenger fish leaping at the falls with all their might, the Wasoga and Waganda fishermen coming out in boats and taking post on all the rocks with rod and hook; hippopotami and crocodiles lying sleepily on the water, the ferry at work above the falls, and cattle down to drink at the margins of the lake—made, in all, with the pretty nature of the country—small hills, grassy-topped, with trees in the folds, and gardens on the lower slopes—as interesting a picture as one could wish to see," he wrote in his journal.

"Though beautiful, the sight was not exactly what I expected, for the broad surface of the lake was shut out from view by the broad surface of a hill," Speke concluded. It would seem a simple matter of connecting the surface of Victoria Nyanza with the powerful torrent spewing forth from its northern lip. But not being able to see both the falls and the lake at the same time added a measure of doubt to the source location. Making matters worse, during his journey from Victoria Nyanza to Cairo, Speke would soon cut a tangent across the African landscape, losing sight of the Nile for days at a time. Dick Burton would later argue that because of these discrepancies, Victoria Nyanza and the Nile were not connected. Strangely enough, many people would believe him.

Yet Speke was convinced he had his proof. "The expedition had now performed its function," he wrote. "I saw that old father Nile without any doubt rises in the Victoria Nyanza, and as I had foretold, that lake is the great source."

Once Speke and Grant pushed north beyond the waterfall spouting forth from Victoria Nyanza, a whole new collection of hostile tribes, religions, and customs needed to be dealt with. There was the constant daily need to feed the porters, keep the caravan happy, and follow the superlative lead of Sidi Mubarak Bombay, the flat-toothed former slave who once again embodied the definition of an explorer by showing them the way.

Speke's first chance to tell the world about the waterfall came on March 27, 1863. He had arrived in the riverfront fortress of Khartoum, where a small garrison of British troops kept the peace. In Khartoum there was also a telegraph line, and a soldier conversant in dots and dashes more than happy to tap out a message back to London from the great explorer John Hanning Speke.

"The Nile," Speke cabled to the RGS, "is settled."

March 27, 1863, was an auspicious date in the history of exploration, though not one the indigenous peoples of Africa and America might ever appreciate.

On that same day, in Washington, DC, President Abraham Lincoln met with chiefs from several prominent Native American tribes. Among them were the Cheyenne, Kiowa, Comanche, Arapahoe, and Apache. The spoken message was a clear wish for peace between the Indian population and the newcomers of mostly European extraction who had charted, encroached upon, and resettled their lands. The unspoken message was that life in America had changed forever, thanks to the discoveries of the American West by the explorers Lewis and Clark between 1804 and 1806. Hat in hand, these proud warriors were being told in no uncertain terms that they lacked the firepower to win the war they were currently pursuing against American settlers.

America, Lincoln was saying in not so many words, is settled.

At one point, Lincoln even invoked the spirit of exploration by laying his hand upon a globe. "I tell you that there are people here in this wigwam," said America's sixteenth president, referring to the White House, "who have come from other countries a great deal farther off than you have come.

We pale-faced people think that this world is a great, round ball, and we have people here of the pale-faced family who have come almost from the other side of it to represent their nations here and conduct their friendly intercourse with us, as you now come from your part of the round ball."

Whereupon Lincoln asked an academic in the audience to step to the globe and deliver a brief lecture on the history of exploration.

Naysayers point to such moments as proof that exploration is wrong, or arrogant, or heartless, and ought not to be pursued. But Lincoln's speech was none of those. In fact, it was a lesson in realpolitik, spoken by a man known to be thoughtful, reasonable, and compassionate. The history of the world is the history of exploration—and its repercussions. Ever since that first man strolled out of Africa thousands and thousands of years ago, great tribes of people have followed him into the unknown. Inevitably, they came in contact with another tribe. One of two things then took place: either the new tribe supplanted the occupants, or they retreated in the face of a more powerful foe. As heartless as it might appear, Lincoln was just speaking the hard truth to make the transition easier—and save thousands of lives.

Speke's message was about to start that same process in Africa.

There could be no turning back. For the first time in history, Speke had shown it possible to link northern Africa with sub-Saharan Africa. Within thirty short years all of Africa would be carved up by European nations ranging from Germany to Belgium to England. Sadly, this transition would go even less smoothly than in America, which was hardly smooth at all. Wars, slavery, mutilations, genocide, and reprisals would continue to mark the relationship between Europeans and Africans for years to come—and still do to this day.

None of this was obvious, however, as Speke's message flashed to London. Murchison passed it along in an address to the RGS, telling them with great confidence that the "problem of all ages" had been solved.

Soon enough Speke and Grant arrived in Cairo, where they experienced the luxury of the Shepheard Hotel* and arranged for ocean passage home for themselves and their porters. On June 17, 1863, Speke and Grant returned to England after an absence of three years, stepping off yet another P&O steamer (the *Pera*)† in Southampton as triumphant heroes. In

---

*Built in 1841 by Englishman Samuel Shepheard, it was for a time the most celebrated hotel in Cairo. Situated on lush grounds that Napoleon's army used as its headquarters during his invasion of Egypt, its many visitors included T. E. Lawrence, Henry Morton Stanley, Theodore Roosevelt, the Prince of Wales, King Faisal of Iraq, the Aga Khan, and Winston Churchill. The original structure burned down in 1952 during civil unrest relating to the Egyptian revolution. Rebuilt at a new site in 1957, it was prominently featured in the Academy Award–winning 1996 film *The English Patient*.

†There were three Peninsular and Oriental steamers named SS *Pera*, and all found unique ways to sink. The first was rechristened the *Alma* almost as soon as she left the shipyard in 1855. She ran aground off Jabal Zugar Island in the Red Sea on December 6, 1859, sinking in 40

keeping with the understated manner of all British exploration, and in continuance of the stiff upper lip with which
Speke had masqueraded for almost three years, there was little
fanfare. Emotional dockside family reunions, complete with
flowers and tears and hugs, were nowhere to be seen.

Too bad.

Dick Burton was not in England at the time. He had
begun his new career as a minor diplomat on the unsavory
West African island of Fernando Po,* and was not inclined to
return home as a welcoming party. Bitter to the end, he had
not let go of his hatred for Speke. Burton, so recently spun
from exploration wunderkind to has-been thanks to the man
he had so severely underestimated, was as eager as ever to
disprove any geographical theories that Speke might set forth.

Now that Speke had returned to civilization, it would
seem that his dependence on self-discipline would no longer

---

feet of water with the loss of one life. The second SS *Pera*, and the one
on which Speke and Grant sailed, was also launched in 1855. The P&O
sold it in 1880 to William Ross & Co. out of Belfast, who put it into Atlantic service. On October 6, 1882, she hit an iceberg off St. Mary's Bay
in Newfoundland. The entire crew was rescued by the nearby schooner
Florella and the SS *Lake Manitoba*. Perhaps thinking the name cursed,
the P&O launched no more *Pera*s until 1903. However, she was also
sent to the bottom in 1917 by the German submarine *UB-48*, helmed
by Captain Wolfgang Steinbauer, while transporting coal from Liverpool
to Calcutta. The wreck can be found in the Mediterranean, 105 miles
north of the Libyan port of Marsa Susa.
*Now known as Bioko, it is 19 miles off the coast of Cameroon, in the
equatorial Gulf of Guinea.

be required. Ironically, after three years in Africa, the trait of self-discipline would never be more necessary. Burton was keen to attack Speke's one true weakness: his intellect. And the mere fact that Speke had not followed each and every mile of that waterfall's course after it flowed out of Victoria Nyanza gave Burton hope that his own arguments about Tanganyika might be proven—that somehow, the outflow Speke had followed to the sea actually began in Tanganyika.

Presenting the world a stiff upper lip was not enough anymore. Now Speke needed to endure—to persevere. Or, as Nile duel moderator David Livingstone liked to say, Speke would need to "Bash on, regardless."

Perseverance, this seventh and final trait of the explorers, takes Speke out of the abstract of the wilderness and places him in the context of real life. As we'll soon see, it's sometimes easier to risk death in some unexplored land than to persevere with all the slings and arrows that come from personal attacks, bad relationships, and public criticism.

In August 1864, Richard Francis Burton finally returned to London. His satchel contained his usual palette of darkness and retribution. So it was that the long, strange duel between Speke and Burton was about to end.

Badly.

PERSEVERANCE

If you find yourself going through hell, keep going.

—Winston Churchill

1

Viewers of the popular BBC television series *Downton Abbey* are well acquainted with the sprawling English country house that appears in the show's opening credits and gives the series its name. The architect was Sir Charles Barry, who remodeled an existing home on the property immediately after he had overseen the building of the Houses of Parliament in 1839. The Jacobethan* design shares the same high towers as that iconic structure on the Thames, giving it the stately appear-

*A blend of Tudor and Renaissance styles. The surrounding grounds were designed by the renowned British landscape architect Capability Brown.

ance that made it the perfect site to locate a modern-day show about the bygone days of British estates and the people who lived and worked there.

There was, of course, no Lord Grantham. Nor was there a Lady Grantham. But the building that doubles for Downton is an actual mansion, rather than a theatrical facade. The home sits on land that has belonged to the Earl of Carnarvon's family since 1692. Its real name is Highclere Castle, and it is germane to this chapter because within those walls exists a museum that testifies to the enormous power of perseverance. Appropriately, the saga behind the museum was played out along the banks of the Nile.

It all began in 1901, when irrepressible George Edward Stanhope Molyneux Herbert—also known as the fifth Earl of Carnarvon—was badly injured in a driving accident. Lord Carnarvon was thirty-five at the time, and notorious for his reckless lifestyle, which included ownership in racehorses and a fondness for driving too fast in that brand-new invention known as the automobile.* The one great enduring image of the earl is a painting that sums up his personality at a glance:

---

*First conceptualized by Jesuit missionary Ferdinant Verbiest, the modern automobile was invented by Karl Benz in 1878, who patented his first engine in 1879 and the Motorwagen design in 1885. It featured three spoked wheels and an open carriage. A fellow German engineer named Gottlieb Daimler was also experimenting with automobile designs at that time. He died in 1900, but his design company, DMG, lived on, producing the vehicle known as the Mercedes in 1902. After World War I the Benz and Daimler corporations were merged. Mercedes-Benz unfiltered cigarette burning between two fingers of his right hand, broad-brimmed Homburg worn at a rakish angle, a confident clipped mustache, and lips pursed in what initially appears to be a smirk, until you see that they are counterbalanced by tired eyes. "Motor" Carnarvon's driving habits were radical enough that he appeared before the local magistrate on several occasions to explain why a man needed to travel at the extraordinary rate of twenty miles per hour. *The Autocar* periodical marveled that he drove "like a flash."

The accident was nearly fatal and highly regrettable for a wealthy playboy man in the prime of his life, but it could not have been unexpected. Nonetheless, the aftereffects were dramatic. During his subsequent recovery, the nearly six-foot-tall Carnarvon shriveled to just 114 pounds. The great drafty corridors of Highclere and the damp British winters became unbearable, so he took to wintering in Egypt. But Carnarvon quickly grew bored in sultry Cairo. Searching for a way to pass the time, he traveled south down the river to Luxor, and began a search for ruins of ancient Egyptian civilization—or Egyptology, as it is known.

This is where exploration comes full circle. Just as with the Leakey excavations in Olduvai Gorge, this process of traveling back to early civilizations is as much about reconnecting the peoples of the world as traveling into new and uncharted

---

is its trademark, but not the company name. The actual corporation is now known as Daimler AG.

lands. This is the Indiana Jones form of exploration, a dazzling world of treasure, history, and intrigue that requires the explorer to piece together the story of a bygone time by finding its bowls and amulets and stone carvings, then figuring out what they mean. This is no different than Burton's ethnography or Cook describing Antarctic ice for the first time. The trick is to find out what was myth and what was real, because the archaeologist is not an eyewitness, but a reconstructor.

Visits to those great museums in London, New York, Cairo, and other assorted cities that house Egyptian artifacts make it appear as if these shards of history were simply plucked from the desert floor and driven straight to the display case. There is such an enormous supply of them, from so many eras and dig sites, that this seems the only logical conclusion. But nothing could be farther from the truth. Centuries of shifting sands and civilizations built atop other civilizations mean that Egyptology is perhaps the most labor-intensive and boring form of exploration ever contrived. The results are sexy, but the nine to five of the task is not. Suffice to say that Lord Carnarvon did not show up for work each morning with a handgun and a bullwhip. He spent each night at the lavish Winter Palace Hotel,* crossed the Nile in the morning by sailboat, was driven across the desert into the range of low mountains that concealed a burial site known as

*The Winter Palace is still as lavish and well maintained one century later. Even if one does not spend the night at the Winter Palace, no visit to Luxor is complete without a walk through the lobby and gardens.

the Valley of the Kings, and then entered a special screened cage that kept the flies away while allowing him to watch teams of hired Egyptian diggers sift shovels full of dry desert sand in the hopes of finding something resembling an artifact. The excitement came from the constant daily hope that one of those diggers would overturn a spade of earth that would reveal a pharaoh's tomb. For the great Egyptian rulers were always buried with their earthly possessions. A good tomb could yield a fortune in gold, ivory, and precious antiquities. And while Lord Carnarvon had no financial concerns, he craved the adrenaline rush and celebrity of that one great discovery.

At the same time, there lived in Egypt a struggling young Briton searching for the same elusive find. Self-educated and lacking much of a future in England, Howard Carter had a talent for sketching and watercolors that led to his being hired to do pen-and-ink drawings of an Egyptian dig site at the precocious age of seventeen. Carter took to Egypt, and developed a passion for all things Egyptological. He soon became an expert on ancient Egyptian civilizations.

Over time, Carter also became what can only be described as a determined failure. He was priggish, self-righteous, and arrogant; an archaeological gigolo who hired out his excavation services to whichever wealthy suitor owned a legitimate claim to dig in the Valley of the Kings. When money was tight he eked out a living selling watercolors in front of the Winter Palace. Through it all, Carter was an idealist. He remained steadfast in the belief that there was still one great undiscovered tomb in the Valley of the Kings—and that one day he would be the man to find it.

"The Valley of the Kings" has such a regal and majestic sound that upon first visit one finds it hard to reconcile that title's intended splendor with the landscape's stark emptiness and the intense desert heat. There is nothing inviting about the terrain, which is precisely why the ancient Egyptians buried their pharaohs in its crags. This was to discourage grave robbers while also providing a true resting place. Very often, slaves were paid to carve a tomb out of the desert rock, then killed upon completing the job so that they would never whisper a word about its location.

The Valley of the Kings now houses a parking lot, a visitor center, and a number of large tombs into which one can walk. Their entrances are so large that Howard Carter often took refuge from the sun and heat inside these very tombs during his workday, eating his lunch at a large table placed inside the entrance for that very purpose.

But let's say you're not visiting the Valley of the Kings in modern times. Let's say you're there a century ago, when the road from the Nile was unpaved and the Valley of the Kings was in the early stages of revealing its secrets. You would be looking at nothing but mounds of rocks and dirt, you would be sweating profusely from the unbearable heat, you would do just about anything for sunblock and a floppy hat to keep the sun off your face, and you would slowly be driven insane by the constant action of swatting away the swarms of flies that torment one and all who visit the valley.

But you do all of this because you know that somehow, beneath one of those piles of desert flotsam, is a tomb. And that finding the tomb might make you rich. So you dig and dig and dig, aided by an army of local men. You do this for a year, maybe two, before realizing that the mound into which you are digging contains no tomb at all. In fact, it contains nothing but dirt and more dirt.

So you dig someplace else. This goes on for another year or two. Maybe you find something, maybe you don't. Maybe that thing you pluck out of the dirt is just an ancient piece of broken pottery, which is immediately scrutinized and analyzed: does it belong to a pharaoh? Or was it left here by a tomb robber 1,000 years ago?

2

I once traveled thousands of miles to stand in the Valley of the Kings. I'd read up on its history, and knew the location of several key tombs—some of which I had to hunch down to squeeze into, and others into which I strolled upright. After a good six hours in the Valley of the Kings I felt like I'd experienced something profound. It was beautiful in its austerity, magical for its timelessness, overwhelming in the harshness of its climate, stunning in the way the clearest imaginable blue sky contrasted so sharply with the dun-colored cliffs and crags; and how, viewed from a trail high atop the valley floor, the distant slithering Nile and the carpet of greenery lining each of its banks contrasted so vividly with the utter nothingness of desert stretching out in all directions.

In a word, the Valley of the Kings was exceptional.

But by the time my wife and I piled into our taxi for the trip back to Luxor, I had seen all I wanted to see. Ever. I don't feel any need to return to the Valley of the Kings.

But Howard Carter returned. Day after day after day, year after year after year, scraping at the earth, standing around for hours in the heat, directing diggers into one pile of rock after another, perhaps growing bored but never losing hope in his gut belief that there was more to be found. He teamed up with Lord Carnarvon in 1907, and used the earl's financing to dig for that elusive tomb. Carter toiled in the valley for so many years that his task became Sisyphean. He dug through the entire valley, finding jars and small tombs and statuary, but the impoverished Carter never found the big payday that would allow him to live out his life in comfort. By 1921, when Carter was forty-seven, Egyptology was falling out of favor in England. World War I had sobered the nation. What had once been a stimulating series of discoveries on par with the poles and the source no longer fascinated the nation—mostly because it appeared that there was nothing left to find. And even Carnarvon was tired of pouring money into excavations. Clearly, the Valley of the Kings had been worked out. It was no different than a gold miner who realizes that his claim will yield no more treasure. The earl summoned Carter to Highclere Castle to give him the bad news that he was giving up—there would be no more digging.

Carter begged for one last chance. There was a small triangle of land in the valley that had never been excavated. Carter was so insistent that Lord Carnarvon was swayed. Thus the digging continued, and on the Wednesday morning of November 1, 1922, Carter found the location of King Tutankhamen's tomb. King Tut, as it became known, was a virgin find, full of the dazzling wealth Carter and Carnarvon had long been seeking. There has never been a greater discovery in the history of archaeology. Everyone got rich. People around the world were suddenly awash in a resurgent passion for Egyptology.

All because Carter and Carnarvon wouldn't quit. All those years of perseverance paid off. The results can be viewed in museums such as the exhibit within Highclere dedicated to the earl's collection of artifacts discovered during the years he indulged his passion for Egyptology.*

---

*Lord Carnarvon died just five months after the discovery of Tut's tomb. He had traveled to Egypt to see it for himself, where he was bitten on the cheek by a mosquito carrying the deadly *erisypelas* bacteria. Carnarvon mistakenly shaved over the bite. It became infected, and he succumbed to pneumonia on April 5, 1923, at the Continental Savoy Hotel in Cairo. His death gave rise to rumors of a suspected curse related to the opening of King Tut's tomb. Others affected by the alleged curse were Carter's pet canary, which was eaten by a cobra on the day the tomb was opened; and Carnarvon's three-legged terrier, which is said to

So ends the Victorian Age of Discovery. What began with the death of Captain James Cook ended with the discovery of King Tut. It was a span of 143 years. During that time, the poles were settled, the source of the Nile was located, the Amazon and her many tributaries were unveiled, North America's peaks and great canyons were measured, the Pacific islands were knit together like so many squares of fabric in a great oceanic quilt, vast and barren Australia was traversed north to south—and east to west, and circumnavigated, making it the first time in history that the mainland of a continent had been so thoroughly explored—and the great hidden mountains of the Asian subcontinent were located and verified as the world's tallest. Men such as Sir Francis Younghusband crossed the Gobi Desert and bridged the divide between India and China, setting forth a great game of geopolitical cat and mouse that almost led to war with Russia, thus confirming what everyone had known all along: as bold and adventurous as the explorers might have been, exploration and empire went hand in hand.

Everest had not yet been climbed on the morning when Howard Carter first saw "wonderful things" gleaming inside Tut's small tomb,* but British mountaineers were sniffing around its edges, searching for a path to the roof of the world.

---

have howled and dropped dead at the exact moment the earl died. Carnarvon is buried on a hill overlooking Highclere Castle.
*Some of the more prominent tombs in the Valley of the Kings have the cavernous feel of a parking garage. Tut's is the size of a studio apartment.

And though man had not yet set foot on the moon, the pro-
gression from first flight to biplane to single-wing propeller to
jets to rockets was already ongoing. Truth be told, all that was
left was for a then-twelve-year-old Jacques Cousteau to invent
the Aqua-Lung so that mankind could venture into the depths
of the oceans—most of which remain uncharted to this day.

3

There will be other discoveries as the Amazon, Africa, and
Antarctica are penetrated deeper, and the subsequent findings
of Louis Leakey about the origins of man in the Olduvai Gorge
take the story right back to that first intrepid explorer who
wandered away from his village one day and then kept right
on walking. But as the RGS would note soon enough by the
sort of undertaking they rewarded when bestowing their gold
medal, the glory days of global exploration were at an end.

Each discovery in the 143 years between Cook and Carter
was powerful in its own right. Yet one stood out above the
rest. One, more than any other, defined Victorian exploration:
Speke's discovery of the Nile's source. The subsequent debate
about the veracity of his findings only added to the drama.

On September 19, 1909, the *New York Times* reflected
back on the Burton and Speke argument as a reference point
when another such disagreement reared its head. "The Peary-
Cook controversy, which promises to occupy people's minds
for some time to come," the paper wrote in reference to duel-

ing claims between Frederick Cook and Robert Peary over who reached the North Pole first.* "Fifty years ago something similar agitated all those interested in exploration. It lasted for years, with ever increasing feelings of bitterness on both sides, and was not definitely settled until one of the principals had died."

As the *Times* suggests, the same perseverance that leads a man to walk through the wilderness for years on end, or use a toothbrush to softly bristle away the sands of time (literally) to excavate a pharaoh's tomb, transferred itself into the grudge

---

*The coincidentally named Cook also claimed to have been the first man to summit Mount McKinley. Both claims were later proven false. It's interesting to note that Cook was also a good friend of Roald Amundsen, whose own journey to the North Pole may likely have been the first, instead of Peary's. As for Mount McKinley, this highest North American peak was originally named Denali by the native Koyukon Athabascan tribe that inhabited the region. During Russia's occupation of Alaska (from early in the nineteenth century until October 18, 1867, thanks to Seward's Purchase; that calendar date is also famous for being the birthday of Lee Harvey Oswald, in 1939) the name was altered to Bolshaya Gora (Great Mountain). However, a supporter of William McKinley renamed it in the then president's honor at the turn of the twentieth century, which it remains to this day. The state of Alaska has reverted to Denali, but congressmen from McKinley's home state of Ohio have blocked requests to make the change official on the United States Board on Geographic Names. Yes, there is such an august body. The BGN was created in 1890 by order of President Benjamin Harrison. Its purpose is to determine and maintain standard usage of geographic names, and its decisions are binding to all of the federal government's agencies and departments. This quiet powerhouse also holds sway over place names in Antarctica and below the ocean surface.

match that became Burton and Speke's geographical pas de deux.

What triggers perseverance? Pleasure. Or, more accurately, the hit of dopamine that the brain releases when an action produces a positive result. On an immediate level, this is the whoosh of an orgasm that prompts the male of the human species to duplicate the reaction. Individuals who perform great feats of perseverance find the same pleasure in the act of work or the small triumphs that accompany a long-term trial. This, in turn, boosts confidence, which triggers a dopamine release. The amount is not the same flash flood as an orgasm, but is enough to appeal to the prefrontal cortex (the brain's logical thinking center) and convince it that continuing this act is a rational idea. This simple act of continuation constitutes perseverance.

If the process of achieving goals ceases at some point, so does the secretion of dopamine. This is why we often abandon a demanding or long-term process. Or, in terms of explorers, the lack of a discovery forced many men and women to turn back. The great explorers endured long spells with little success, but continued to press forward because they found pleasure in the experience, and also because their hopes for a great success propelled them toward their goals. For in that hope came the promise of the dopamine release—and perhaps in a flash flood far more extraordinary and long-lasting than the buzz of an orgasm.

Think of John Hunt's euphoric comments after leading

the 1953 Everest expedition. And also think of men such as the Olympic swimmer Michael Phelps, who endured years of staring at that black line on the bottom of the pool in the hopes of winning an Olympic medal. In peak phases of training, he swam 50 miles a week. This came to 6 hours a day in the water, along with three times a week in the weight room doing dry land training. The focus of all that work was a competition that occurs only once every four years. There were smaller meets in between, such as the world and national championships, but that Olympic gold is the be-all and end-all of the swimming world. An athlete's legacy depends upon the color and number of medals. Over the course of three Olympics (2004, 2008, 2012), Phelps won twenty-two, of which eighteen were gold. This is the most ever won by any athlete in Olympic history, in any sport. The dopamine release that came with each victory must have been enormous, overwhelming the naysayer portion of the brain (ventromedial prefrontal cortex) that might have suggested he not devote his life to such a goal, or even hope that he would achieve something so grandiose.

We're not all going to discover the source. Just as we're not all going to win an Olympic gold medal. But there is great inspiration in these moments when human beings push themselves beyond the limits of mediocrity, in the process achieving a sublime glory that most of us experience rarely or never at all. This is one of the reasons why athletes cry during their national anthem. Standing atop the podium, mind and body numbed by dopamine, they realize that their perseverance has paid off. Part relief, part disbelief, it is one of those ultimate highs that life does not proffer easily. I suspect, though this is just a guess, that the reason entire nations bond together while watching the Olympics, learning the names of athletes from small, neglected sports and shedding tears of utter happiness when they triumph, is because their success offers us all a taste of that transcendence. Life is hard, and offers few chances to rise above the ruts and snares that cause us to settle for less than our personal best. But by watching others experience greatness, we know a little bit of that, too. It's why we become inspired by the Olympic Games, or any other moment of spectacular accomplishment. It's the emotional adhesive that resonates within our brains, making us think that we can attempt something just a little bit great—not Olympian, but something on a modest personal level—that will provide that same euphoria. There's dopamine aplenty in training for a marathon, writing a page per day on that long-neglected novel, or performing any of a number of feats that propel you outside your comfort zone.

So don't quit. And when a task becomes difficult and the lack of dopamine makes it hard to push forward, remember that perseverance can be learned. It's as simple as (1) taking a hard look at any new goal that has presented itself; (2) realistically believing that the goal is attainable; (3) begin working toward that goal (initial whoosh of dopamine just for moving forward!); (4) establishing milestones for motivation when times get tough; (5) being unafraid of veering away from the initial plan in order to realize a goal (with the new whoosh of dopamine that comes with owning the process); (6) accepting the mental and physical hardships that come with chasing this new dream; and (7) continuing to push forward.

"Never give up. Never give up. Never ever, ever, ever give up," Winston Churchill once said.

Because to quit, or to have hope turn to despair, can produce low levels of the chemical serotonin. This is the opposite of dopamine, and can plunge an individual into a deep trench of depression that seems to have no bottom.

4

So it was with Jack Speke. He returned to England after not only making a profound and monumental discovery, but also accomplishing a journey that mankind had long dreamed of; an act of perseverance begun by countless men down through the centuries, all of whom quit before it was completed. It is safe to assume that Speke expected two things: fame and peace of mind. The former would come through formal recognition by the British government, perhaps in the form of a knighthood. The peace of mind would come through widespread acceptance that he had pinpointed the source of the Nile, once and for all. This would forever put an end to his quarrels with Dick Burton, and ensure that there would be no further attempts to discredit his discovery.

Alas, neither was to be. Lord Palmerston,* the aged British prime minister, thought so little of Speke's incredible journey that he ignored Sir Roderick Murchison's barrage of pleas that Speke be knighted. This wouldn't have been such a slight, if Palmerston didn't also manage to cast doubt on Speke's discovery by writing that "The question arises whether there are not other African explorers, as for instance Livingstone . . . who could make such a claim" as to the source's true location.

Palmerston did make it possible for the Speke family to add a hippopotamus and crocodile to their coat of arms as a symbol of Speke's journey, but Palmerston's public dismissal of Victoria Nyanza as the source had a snowball effect. Murchison was overwhelmingly fond of Livingstone, thinking him the greatest of his "lions," as he called those RGS explorers specializing in the African continent. His allegiance to Speke went nowhere near as deep. The seed of doubt planted by Palmerston soon took hold.

Speke then unwittingly broadened the gap when he authorized a publisher to turn his journals into a book. To ensure that the words would draw the greatest possible sales from the reading public, he did not excerpt or write a synopsis for inclusion in the RGS's in-house journals. Speke didn't help

---

*Palmerston's palatial London home still looks out over Piccadilly and Green Park. However, it has fallen into disrepair, and sits in a pathetic shamble just a few blocks from the Duke of Wellington's own monumental home, waiting for someone with a great deal of time and money to restore it.

matters by publicly stating that John Petherick, a Welshman whom the RGS had enlisted to resupply Speke in the Sudan during his journey, had profited from the slave trade while in Africa. And then Speke went one better, and opened old wounds by beginning work on a second book about Africa. This one would be based on his journey with Burton, but this time telling Speke's side of the story.

Speke most likely experienced a dopamine boost with these acts of defiance, but his perseverance in the matter of the source soon took on a bitter quality. Rather than setting aside his geographical debate with Burton, whom he hadn't seen in years, Speke wrote to friends about "the amount of injustice he has done to me," and fumed about getting revenge.

Speke's rapid tumble from grace continued. From national hero and much-admired Nile conqueror, Speke descended from favor with Murchison, then slowly saw the possibilities of his new dream of an east-to-west expedition across Africa dwindle due to this new political isolation. He then made matters far worse by meeting with French emperor Napoleon III in August of 1864, hoping to secure funding for the journey. Explorers were well known for exploiting any avenue to pay for a new journey, and even under the best of circumstances they were not only poorly funded—even by the RGS—but also held accountable for every expenditure. The 1834 RGS gold medal recipient William Ross, the man who endured four winters in the Arctic, paid for that expedition through an endowment from a gin distiller named Felix

Booth. Not only did he Latinize his discovery and name the new land Boothia Felix, but the name stuck—and is quoted to this day as part of Ross's gold medal pronouncement.* So in the absence of financial support from the British government or the RGS, Speke was well within his rights to court outside investors.

But Speke was landed gentry, born into a family that had maintained an estate on English soil for centuries. He was thought to be a proper Victorian gentleman, not a mercenary. And while Speke may have felt simmering outrage about not being knighted, there was something extremely distasteful about taking his financial concerns to the French, of all people.

As it has been well documented, the British and French have disliked one another to an extreme degree for a thousand years. Speke's indiscretion was an act that effectively severed, at least temporarily, the goodwill between himself, the RGS, and those members of the British establishment paying attention to such matters. Given that the RGS worked closely with the British Foreign Office to ensure that exploration was soon after followed by colonization or some other incursion designed to capitalize on a region's assets, Speke's behavior

*Now known as the Boothia Peninsula, it is in the Canadian Arctic, just south of Somerset Island. The northern portion of the Boothia Peninsula has also been renamed. It is now known as Murchison Promontory, in honor of Sir Roderick. There are fifteen geographical locations on Earth named in the RGS president's honor. There is one other place named for the once-wastrel Scot. It is called simply "Murchison," and is a crater next to the Sinus Medii on the moon.

could only have been seen as an act of betrayal, if not trea-son. The mere thought of the French taking over Britain's hard-won—and RGS-backed—lands in Africa must have sent Sir Roderick Murchison into a state of apoplexy.

The same lack of discretion that would soon prove the de-mise of Livingstone, and had once been the downfall of Cap-tain Cook, had burrowed into Speke's more rational veneer. Rather than the great hero who had endured two heinous expeditions into Africa, Speke became a villain.

So it was interesting when Sir Roderick did something that was either incredibly cruel or incredibly kind: he invited Speke to the resort city of Bath, where a debate over the source of the Nile would take place as part of the British As-sociation for the Advancement of Science's meeting. On one side would be Dr. David Livingstone, newly returned from an expedition of his own to the Zambezi that had not only gone poorly, but had resulted in a number of deaths—including that of his wife. His job was to appear resolute and learned, rather than as the crazed martinet that some from the expedi-tion were now portraying him. At age fifty-one, his body play-ing host to a number of African parasites that he would never shake, Livingstone was now the elder statesman of RGS ex-plorers. The former missionary was not at all happy that a new generation of explorers was making discoveries of significantly greater public interest.

And while Livingstone remained passionate in his belief that the Zambezi River was the greatest of all African waterways, the hard truth was that the British people were much more curious about the source of the Nile—which bothered Livingstone no end. And there was nothing he could do about it. The outcome of the debate would establish once and for all the true source of the Nile. Livingstone's beloved Zambezi would be relegated to second-tier status.

Livingstone's role as moderator was meant by Murchison to help restore some of the former missionary's august reputation. And while Livingstone was too proud and far too independent to consider his appearance in Bath as an act of public contrition, that's exactly what it was. Because there was every chance that the Zambezi expedition had been Livingstone's last.

Burton would also be standing on the speaker's platform. Speke had somehow managed to offend almost everyone associated with British exploration by then, and in particular, the saintly Livingstone, who was feeling more and more proprietary about Africa. Thus the deeply Christian David Livingstone stood to be the ally of Muslim-centric Dick Burton during the Nile duel—a brotherhood that came together only because both men despised Speke just slightly more than they loathed one another.

The arguments between Burton and Speke were meant to take place in the Royal Mineral Water Hospital in the heart of Bath. The building still exists, and if you can distract the orderly at the front desk, as my wife once did so that I might get a glimpse—or perhaps, simply ask permission—it's possible to venture inside and get a feel for what "the Min"—as it is informally known—must have been like on September 16, 1864. The regal building with the faux-columned exterior has the timeless appearance of a facility whose foundation stone was first laid in 1738, and is still very much in business. A direct hit from a German bomb destroyed portions of it in 1942, and an extensive modernization project in 1962 revamped much of the interior. The gist of the Royal Mineral Water Hospital is its stately grandeur. In every way, it was an ideal location to settle the matter of the Nile. The fact that a divisive geographic riddle about the precise location where water spewed from the Earth would be debated inside a facility that owed its existence to the healing power of a natural spring could only have been Sir Roderick Murchison's idea of a fine inside joke.

So the crowds of the learned, the curious, and those fond of dramatic spectacle took the train from London to Bath as the weekend approached, then lined up outside the Min on that wet September morning. Their wool and fur coats must have smelled horribly from the rain, and the clamor for tickets into the sold-out debate would have made for a growing excitement. The Nile Debate—the "Nile duel," as many also called it, rightly guessing that one man would emerge victorious and the other all but dead to British society—would be the undoubted dramatic conclusion to a drama that had been escalating for almost a decade.

Little did those thousands of spectators realize, but the

Nile duel's final moments would be far more explosive than any man or woman in that crowded, damp, overflowing hall could possibly imagine.

5

The outcome, in fact, had already been decided.

It happened the night before, in the sedate autumn fields of Neston Park. Standing just 60 yards from his cousin Jack Speke as the two men hunted birds, George Fuller turned toward the sound of a muffled shotgun blast.

At the exact same instant, one hundred small round pellets of #8 lead birdshot ripped through Jack Speke's torso.

George Fuller watched his cousin topple off the low stone wall over which he'd been climbing just a moment earlier. The Lancaster shotgun with the Damascus steel barrels fell harmlessly to the ground. One round was still chambered. George and Daniel Davis, the gamekeeper assisting with the hunt, sprinted to Speke. The explorer was collapsed on the grass and moaning. His body lay parallel to the wall, right next to the Lancaster. The shotgun's empty left barrel and its right barrel were still at half cock. Blood flowed from the gaping entry wound on the front of Speke's body and the large exit wound on his back, making small crimson puddles in the dying grass that grew larger and more troubling by the instant.

George Fuller pressed his palm down hard on the great explorer's chest, desperately applying pressure to stop the bleeding. There was no sound. No conversation. Just three men in an empty field as the unseen sun dropped lower and lower in the sky. It soon became apparent that Jack Speke might die on this obscure patch of soil. Not alongside hundreds of other men on the great battlefields of India and the Crimea upon which he once fought for God and country. And not in the teeth of a crocodile. Speke would never be dismembered by a hostile tribe, driven to insanity by an insect lodged in his ear, or once again racked by malaria.

In fact, as he lay bleeding on the grass, those years on the Nile counted for very little to John Hanning Speke. The Nile duel meant even less.

Richard Francis Burton's geographical posturing meant nothing at all.

"Don't move me," Speke insisted.

He was lying on British soil, among people who loved him as family, wearing comfortable hunting tweeds and expensive boots of soft leather.

Five minutes passed. Speke began to lose consciousness. George Fuller ordered Daniel Davis to place his own hands over his cousin's wounds to stanch the bleeding. After wiping his bloody hands on the grass, George ran hard back to the house to call for Dr. Snow, the surgeon living in the nearby town of Box. It was a desperate race against time. With any luck, Dr. Snow might be at Speke's side within the hour—if Speke could last that long.

Snow arrived to find Speke precisely where he had fallen,

a wound on the left side of his body "such as would be made by a cartridge if the muzzle of the gun was close to the body. It led in a direction upwards and toward the spine, passing through the lungs and dividing all the large blood vessels near the heart."

But Dr. Snow reached the scene far too late. Speke stopped breathing just fifteen minutes after the Lancaster blew a hole in his torso.

John Hanning Speke was thirty-seven years old: discoverer of Victoria Nyanza, first man in history to travel from the coast of eastern Africa all the way to the Mediterranean; and, as the Latin inscription on his black marble sarcophagus would soon read, deeply, completely, and unabashedly "Illustrious for the Nile."

If there was a saving grace to his tragic death, it was that Speke was not alone in his final moment, as he might have been had he died in Africa.

He had Daniel Davis there to comfort him on the dying grass of Neston Park as he breathed his last.

In this way, John Hanning Speke died in the arms of a fellow explorer.

6

Burton took his place first atop the speaker's platform, quietly sitting before the crowd of two thousand curious armchair adventurers. He held in his hands a thick set of arguments in favor of Tanganyika and the Rusizi. As time passed and his opponent failed to appear, rumors spread through the crowd about a delay. By eleven o'clock, the scheduled starting time, the room was nearly manic with excitement. The *Bath Chronicle* reported that "the crowd gave vent to its impatience by sounds more often heard from the audience of a theater than a scientific meeting"—which was appropriate, because the British Association for the Advancement of the Sciences had been infiltrated by a legion of men and women who cared nothing at all about science but everything for the soap opera drama between Burton and Speke.

It was 11:25 when the great wooden doors opened and Sir Roderick Murchison walked somberly to the speaker's platform. "I have to apologize but when I explain to you the cause of my being a little late in coming to take the chair, you will pardon me."

The audience leaned in, desperate to hear his next words.

"Captain Speke," Murchison said solemnly, "has lost his life."

The *Chronicle* reported that "Sensation" roared through the room.

Burton would later note that Speke was a stickler for gun safety, and that "even when our canoe was shaken and upthrown by hippopotamus, he never allowed his gun to look at him or others." The question soon sweeping through the room was one that overshadows Speke's legacy to this day: did he kill himself, or was it an accident? He will be remembered more for the mystery behind his death than for the majesty of the way he lived.

Burton collapsed in his chair, apparently stricken with grief—though not enough to later stand and deliver a treatise dealing with his personal thoughts on exploration. He would still be alive in 1877, when Henry Morton Stanley returned from a 999-day journey across Africa that confirmed Speke's Victoria Nyanza as the premier source of the Nile by proving that the Rusizi River flowed into Lake Tanganyika. This forever erased Burton from the historical record. That fact would be reinforced during the passion-fueled journey of Ewart Grogan from Cape Town to Cairo just before the turn of the twentieth century, when he completed the exploration of the watershed between the Rusizi and Victoria Nyanza that Burton and Speke had been tasked with forty-five years earlier.

Strangely, the cult of Burton would grow and grow. His legend would far eclipse that of Speke. Burton had an antagonistic flair for the dramatic that made him Victorian exploration's rebel without a cause.

Jack Speke was nothing like that. He was an ordinary person accomplishing extraordinary things. Speke was, in other words, the epitome of an explorer. No cult following is necessary to document the fact that he found a way to push his personal limits, step outside his comfort zone, and change the world, however staid and boring he might seem alongside the rage-fueled Burton.

7

Curiosity. Hope. Passion. Courage. Independence. Self-Discipline. Perseverance.

And, of course, the overlooked final trait: Discretion, that cohesive and rational ability to bind each surpassing achievement with a clear sense of perspective. In discretion we see our personal expeditions not as the be-all and end-all of daily existence, but as a form of enrichment that spills over into relationships, outlook, and overall quality of life. Discretion is the art of knowing better. An accumulation of life's wisdoms prevents us from making the same mistake twice, or allows us the forethought to prevent that mistake from happening at all. Research has shown that this rational thought process can be assisted by aerobic exercise—running, long walks, cycling, paddling, and the like. These simple physical acts make changes to our body through the regulation of dopamine and serotonin, acting to reduce impulsivity and encourage wise decision-making.

But discretion is hard to come by once emotional variables enter the picture, no matter how many long walks an individual takes—and African exploration was nothing but a series of very long walks. David Livingstone, for instance, needed three things as the Nile duel came to an abrupt halt: (1) money, because he was broke and had little savings to provide for his children's inheritance; (2) a restoration of his good name as Africa's greatest explorer after his Zambezi debacle; and (3) a newfound desire to be the man who discovered the source of the Nile.

Sir Roderick Murchison came calling soon after the Nile duel came to its unsatisfying conclusion. The great showman prevailed upon Livingstone to undertake one last great expedition into Africa to solve the great unanswered geographical riddle, proving whether it was Burton or Speke who had located the source of the Nile.

This was the journey from which Livingstone got completely lost.

It was also the journey from which he never returned.

The lack of discretion was not that Livingstone undertook one last great adventure in middle age, nor that he abandoned his children forevermore to do so, nor even that he refused to return to civilization after Henry Morton Stanley so famously found the good doctor after years of being lost in the wilderness.

No, the great lack of discretion came from the wizened Livingstone's ego. He ignored the findings of Speke and Burton almost entirely. Instead of focusing his attentions on Lake Tanganyika and Victoria Nyanza, he fixated on his beloved Zambezi as being the source. The fact that he eventually blundered into Ujiji was an act of provenance. From there he could have marched north into that watershed between Tanganyika and Victoria that Burton and Speke had left unexplored. But instead, after being reprovisioned by Stanley, Livingstone once again marched due south to the Zambezi River—and to his death.

8

Jack Speke's career marked the zenith of exploration, a high point from which this calling slowly descended until it doesn't exist at all.

The Neston Park country house and estate still stand. The wall that Speke clambered over can be found just a few hundred yards off A365, or the Bath Road, as it is commonly known.* The fields are pastoral and calming, dotted with organically raised cows and sheep. It is easy to get a sense of why Speke chose that spot to wander and hunt in order to calm himself before doing battle with his archrival.

Perhaps the potential of death by his own hand† is why Murchison chose to erect an obelisk rather than a statue in Speke's likeness to commemorate his passing. Whether or not this is the case, the monument is actually more powerful for not being normal statuary. Look for yourself. It can be found in London's Kensington Gardens, some 300 yards from the Peter Pan statue personally commissioned by author J. M. Barrie.‡

The Speke monument is a towering obelisk carved from red Aberdeen granite. The people of Kensington paid for it

*The Fuller family still owns Neston Park. They are better known for brewing Fuller's London Pride Cask Ale, which remains a staple at pubs throughout England.
†One has only to read *Hamlet* to understand the ageless stigma that would have accompanied Speke's death if, indeed, it was suicide.
‡A coincidence that seems symbolically appropriate, given that explorers are often characterized as individuals unwilling or unable to grow up.

through public subscriptions shortly after his death, and the memorial looks as smooth and unweathered today as when that great Victorian showman Murchison oversaw its unveiling in 1866.* A small wrought-iron fence keeps visitors at arm's length. An inscription on the face of the obelisk reads: "In Memory of Speke, Victoria Nyanza and the Nile."

It's interesting to note that in 1866, nobody was absolutely positive that Speke had truly located the source; thus the lack of the word "discovery" in the inscription. It would seem that the time and trouble of designing and building the monument were just a bit premature. But there it is. Murchison, whether out of a deep distrust of Burton, regret over turning his back on such an accomplished young lion, or a melancholy eagerness to name Speke the winner of the Nile duel, raised the money and had the granite quarried and polished† a decade before it was confirmed that Speke was, in fact, discoverer of the source.

Further complicating matters is the location of the obelisk. It would appear that Speke benefited from his era's passion for Nile exploration. For all the legendary discoveries by the British Empire's legion of adventurers, Speke is the only one honored with a statue in London's most public and well-traveled park. It can be argued that fellow African explorer

---

*Speke's crypt can be found at the Church of St. Andrew at Dowlish Wake.

†Apparently Murchison was quite fond of red Aberdeen granite. He directed that the same rock be used for his tombstone.

David Livingstone or Antarctic hero Ernest Shackleton was
more courageous, or at the very least more intrepid, but their
statues are limited to small vestibules along the brick exterior
of the Royal Geographic Society, just across Kensington Road
from Hyde Park. Even the one man who can lay claim to the
title of "World's Greatest Explorer," Captain James Cook, is
limited to a relatively anonymous location behind the Old
Admiralty Building.* Speke's legacy is the least remembered
of that Murderers' Row of exploration greats.

Nonetheless, there it stands in the sprawling grandeur
of Kensington Gardens, Speke's name boldly etched in that
pillar of polished stone. The absence of his likeness gives the
monument a timeless appearance. We don't glimpse his fussy
Victorian clothing or the floppy felt hunting hat or an artist's
rendition of his long, wispy beard. What we gaze upon instead
is a powerful and tapering four-sided column that comes to
a point at the top, a construct first discovered and named by
the Greek explorer Herodotus in the fifth century BC—while
exploring the Nile, no less—that alludes to a sense of greatness

*Ironically, the Cook statue was unveiled by His Royal Highness Prince
Arthur of Connaught on July 7, 1914—less than a month before the war
that would begin the slow erosion of the empire first begun by Cook's
explorations and continued through the subtle guidance of Connaught's
grandmother, Queen Victoria. Worth noting is that one early and oft-
overlooked battle of World War I took place on the shores of Bagamoyo,
on the same flat, sandy beach where the Burton and Speke Expedition
began.

and imagination. Small wonder that obelisks are used more often than any other shape as a remembrance of explorers.*

So in a way, it is not Speke whom the monument honors, but the spirit of exploration. Standing before it on a raw February morning, reading exotic words about "the Nile" and "Victoria Nyanza" is to be swept away on a wave of possibilities. A flickering spirit of adventure makes the mind wander. Images of a mighty river, a barren desert, deadly crocodiles, and a sultry African dawn whisk the reader away from cosmopolitan London, if only temporarily.

And of a lone explorer, striving against all odds to accomplish something considered impossible, if only because his life will not be complete until he does so.

9

The history of exploration is a vivid record of ordinary people doing extraordinary things. Jack Speke wouldn't have described his career in that fashion, nor would most anyone who tramped through the wilderness or sailed the 100-foot waves of the Southern Ocean to unveil those dark spots on the map

*The most intriguing use of an obelisk is the Herndon Monument on the grounds of the US Naval Academy in Annapolis, Maryland. Named for Captain William Herndon, who went down with his ship in 1857, the obelisk is coated in lard each spring and scaled by the school's freshman class as a sign that the rigors of their plebe year are behind them. This demanding and somewhat frustrating rite of passage can last as little as forty-five minutes or as long as several hours.

once marked "Unknown." They were just performing a job they enjoyed, that they accomplished with spectacular proficiency, and that would have left them deeply unhappy if they hadn't seen it through to its completion.

But no one remains in the wilderness for life.

"You cannot stay on the mountain forever," wrote René Daumal in *Le Mont Analogue*, his 1952 philosophical exploration of mountaineering. "You have to come down again. So why bother in the first place? Just this: What is above knows what is below, but what is below does not know what is above. One climbs, one sees. One descends, one sees no longer, but one has seen. There is an art of conducting oneself in the lower regions by the memory of what one saw higher up. When one can no longer see, one can at least still know."

So it is that mountain climbers turn their backs on the great peaks. Pilots land one last time. Arctic explorers take off their anoraks. And African explorers only see lions in the zoo.

But that doesn't mean they stop challenging themselves.

The same should be true for us all.

Within each of us beats the heart of an explorer. Though it's true that there are no new continents to be discovered, each of us, just like the explorers, faces a daily barrage of adversity, complication, and decision. Our personal journeys through the wilderness go on each and every day. Within some of us is a mountain climber, within another a brilliant entrepreneur. In our lives we will be faced with great unknowns: the diagnosis of cancer, the call to help a troubled friend, or the need to move forward after tragedy. As professionals we will attempt to chart paths that, however modest our lives may appear on the outside, involve deep moral decisions and complex tactical judgments.

But they are paths into the wilderness we must follow, even if we don't know where they lead and the potential for getting hopelessly lost is enormous.

Because sometimes, as the explorers learned, it is only by getting lost in this wilderness that we find out who we truly are.

AUTHOR'S NOTE

Many years ago, while I was writing a book on the life of Captain James Cook, the noted Australian writer and editor Graem Sims sent me a copy of Wilfrid Noyce's *The Springs of Adventure*. Coincidentally, my good friend Toby Walker also sent me a copy of Noyce's book at the exact same time, so it seemed that the cosmos was trying to tell me something. Noyce was a member of the British team that reached the summit of Everest in 1953, and died after falling 4,000 feet in a climbing accident nine years later.

He writes most eloquently about why mankind feels the pull toward adventure. Noyce was wide-ranging in his examination, discerning the motives of not just mountain climbers, but also desert explorers, sailors, aviators, and pretty much every sort of outdoor adventure that forces mankind to push their mental, physical, and emotional limits. A great number of the quotes and anecdotes in *The Explorers* have been borrowed straight from Noyce's pages, and the subject itself forms the backbone of this book. I began to wonder about not just the emotional motivations to pursue a life of adventure, but the specific character traits that went into being a successful explorer.

These ruminations served as a guide through my trilogy of books about exploration (Cook—Stanley and Livingstone—Columbus), but I could never seem to find a way to blend those traits into a narrative. Lord knows I tried. Some of those earlier attempts to tell that particular story survived and can be seen in the pages of *The Explorers*, but for the most part it was too unwieldy to maintain a strong thread. So I set the idea aside for the better part of ten years as my writing wandered away from the world of exploration. But once I began work on what was originally meant to be a simple retelling of the Burton and Speke saga, it seemed like this book deserved more than just a rote piece of nonfiction exploration storytelling. As I began to write, the experiences of other explorers began noodling their way onto the page, shoving Burton and Speke to the side for paragraphs and pages. The influence of Bill Bryson's *A Short History of Nearly Everything* told me that this should not be a cause for concern, and the neuroscience leanings of Seth Godin showed me that it was possible to use

Burton and Speke as a linchpin for a much greater story. And so I began poking into not just the relevant sagas about other explorers to help flesh out the drama, but also to investigate their character traits.

As you can imagine, the investigation got complicated.

It used to be that when I needed to do a lengthy piece of research, I hopped on a plane and flew to places like London to examine the British Newspaper Archive or the Royal Geographical Society's records. At the very least I would drive to the nearby library at the University of California in Irvine to poke through the stacks. It was always a good excuse for a short adventure and did wonders for my frequent flyer mileage balances. But the onset of the digital age put an end to all that. Some very serious scholarly research can be done from right here in my home office. Thus, as I began to examine the character traits of the explorers, I consulted a number of online papers and research journals. When the academic world became too complex, I could always rely on *Modern Psychology* to explain it in simple terms.

I read and greatly enjoyed the works of thinkers like Seth Godin, Susan Cain, and Michael Gelb. You can find their notions about the lizard brain, introversion, and Da Vinci's creative process in these pages. I urge you to read them in greater detail. It's really super stuff.

I cribbed from those men and women who have spent their lives studying the brain and behavior, and have credited their theories throughout this book where applicable. My approach was to research about the mind and human behavior with the same in-depth focus I would give to unearthing nuggets of information about historical characters. Any conclusions that I have drawn about brain function, the inner workings of the brain, and anything else having to do with that most vital of all organs are the musings of a very fascinated layman. I do not for a second pretend to be the ultimate authority on these matters.

Wandering through theories about Intrinsic Motivation and Self-Efficacy and many others has been a real treat, and I have the greatest admiration for those who pour their passion into it each day. The chapter on self-discipline turned out to be the most enlightening to build, and I found myself most inspired by the research. It should be noted that Mary Boyle, my Ph.D. friend in the Department of Cognitive Science at the University of California at San Diego, was particularly awesome about pointing me toward the latest findings about all aspects of brain function. Even as I write these words, another email just arrived from her directing me to a new study on the unconscious workings of the brain.

As for the historical aspects of this story, there was the typical level of hands-on research, including the journey across Tanzania that I have mentioned in the story, finding the location of the Saturday Club's first meeting, Burton's grave, the Royal Geographical Society archives, and other sites that must be seen in person to be fully appreciated. There's something about standing in a spot and seeing how the sun shines on it, or how the grass smells on an autumn day, that helps to write with greater clarity. There's not a single time that I travel to London and don't stand for a few quiet minutes at the Speke obelisk. It is transcendent, just as Sir Roderick must have hoped a century and a half ago.

I also relied on the research of other writers to find facts that I overlooked or did not fully appreciate in my own wanderings. In particular, the writings of Tim Jeal (*Explorers of the Nile*), Anthony Sattin (*The Gates of Africa*), Alfred Lansing (*Endurance*), Apsley Cherry-Garrard (*The Worst Journey in the World*), Edward Rice (*Captain Sir Richard Francis Burton*), Alan Moorehead (*The White Nile* and *The Blue Nile*), Jan Morris (*Heaven's Command*), Patrick O'Brian (*Joseph Banks*), Julian Smith (*Crossing the Heart of Africa*), and J. C. Beaglehole (*The Life of Captain James Cook*), were all mined for insight. In addition, I relied on my own books (*Into Africa, Last Voyage of Columbus, Farther Than Any Man*) and the many explorers' journals and notes that went into writing them. Not many people take the time to dig into the lives of Burton and Speke. So I should note that I was amused (and validated) to find that many of my own conclusions about Speke and Burton's behavior and emotional connections to the respective lakes that they discovered were mirrored in Jeal's excellent book.

In addition to these works, and a handful of others that did not play as pivotal a role, I relied on the journals of various explorers when it was time to use their own words.

And finally, the footnotes that I have sprinkled so liberally throughout the text are an offshoot of nightly conversations I had with my family at the dinner table. In most households, this is a time of sharing about events of the day. But writing a history book is more about time travel into the events of a day that happened years or centuries ago. So I would invariably wander back inside the house after hours of writing, my head awhirl with crazy nuggets of knowledge and thoughts still pondering Victorian exploration. I would "regale"—my word—my wife and sons with the fascinating bits of historical trivia that had made the time so pleasurable. For the most part, however, they could not be wedged into whichever book I was writing, for fear of weighing down the narrative.

My boys would invariably roll their eyes at my endless parade of "fun facts," but it became a playful tradition of sorts. This is the first book where sharing that tradition with the reader seems to make sense. This is a random collection of facts and factoids, to be sure, destined to clog up the filing cabinets of your gray matter in ways that only become useful when amusing your friends at a cocktail party, playing *Trivial Pursuit* or watching *Jeopardy!* I hope that you have enjoyed them.

ACKNOWLEDGMENTS

Over the course of my career I've had the great honor of working with some of the best editors in publishing: Jason Kaufman, Geoff Shandler, Gillian Blake, and now Jofie Ferrari-Adler and Alessandra Bastagli. Thanks to each of you for your insights and pearls of wisdom.

Special thanks to Alessandra for seeing the merit in the original idea for this book, and to Jofie for enduring its mutations on the path from concept to completed work. It took a very long while, but we got it done.

To super-agent Eric Simonoff, a heartfelt thanks for all you do. You're amazing.

To Bill O'Reilly, a very cool guy from whom I've learned

so much about storytelling, thank you for pushing me to dig deeper and deeper into the research to flesh out a better story.

Thanks to my Mom and Dad. I love you both very much.

Thanks to Ann Butler, the high school English teacher who changed my life by suggesting that I become a writer. And to Chris Noonan, who reminds me that Mrs. Butler's first name is spelled without an "e."

To my sons: Devin, Connor, and Liam, who endured my frequent travels and those countless nights of historical trivia at the dinner table. Thanks for letting me riff.

And to Calene: You are my sunshine.

INDEX

INDEX

Apollo 11, 201
Apollo lunar missions, 206
apoplexy, 25
Apostle Paul, 225
Appalachian Mountains, 30–31
Aqua-Lung, 247
Arabia, 112
Arabs, 110
Arab slave traders, 109
Arctic, 168
Aristotle, 159–60, 168
Armstrong, Neil, 7, 11, 101, 210n
arrogance, 224
Arundel, Isabel, 83, 151, 215
Ascend the Nile, 192
athletes, 250–51
Australia, 31, 40n–41n, 169, 194, 246
  penal colonies in, 36
automobiles, 238n
autonomy, 27
aviation, 205–10

Bagomoyo, 109
Balboa, Vasco Núñez de, 67n
Baltic Sea, 44
baluchis, 110
Bandura, Albert, 222, 224–25
Banks, Joseph, 35–37, 38, 39–42, 45, 46,
  47–48, 81
Barbary pirates, 47
Barrie, J. M., 266
Barry, Charles, 237
Bath Chronicle, 262
beads, 184
Beardmore Glacier, 170, 171
Beatson, W. F., 82, 86
Beaufoy, Henry, 35, 39
Bell, Gertrude, 27
Benz, Karl, 238n
Billings, Joseph, 45
bin Laden, Osama, 165
black mambas, 118
Bligh, William, 36
Blue Nile, 31, 32, 194
Board on Geographic Names, 248n
Bobonaza River, 74
Bogota, 178
boma, 117
Bombay, 27
Bombay, Sidi Mubarak, 109, 153, 153n,
  220, 231

Bonpland, Aimé, 175–79
boomslang, 118
Boone, Daniel, 30–31, 32
Booth, Felix, 254
Boothia Peninsula, 255n
Borman, Frank, 18
Boston Watch Company, 120
Botany Bay, 40n–41n
Bounty, 36
Bowers, Henry, 173, 174
Brendan the Navigator, St., 58–59, 60–61,
  66, 75, 91, 102, 210
  death of, 62
  Prayer of, 57–58
Briga (St. Brendan's sister), 62
British Admiralty, 93
British Association for the Advancement
  of Science, 84, 256, 262
British Empire, 34, 84, 85, 122
British Foreign Office, 255
British Special Air Service (SAS), 162–63
brothels, 24–25
Bruce, James, 31, 32, 38
buffalo hunters, 21–22
buffalo hunting, 21–22
Burke, Edmund, 38
Burroughs, Edgar Rice, 113
Burton, Richard Francis, 2, 12, 23, 24–26,
  42, 46, 50–51, 55–56, 59, 64, 76–77,
  80, 81–82, 85, 86, 87–88, 103,
  104–5, 106, 107, 115, 140, 146–47,
  148, 180–81, 183, 195, 197–98, 201,
  212–13, 215, 221, 231, 236, 240,
  249, 252, 257, 260, 261–62, 263, 267
  army career of, 24–25
  in attempts to discredit Speke, 213
  Barbera attack on, 52–53
  Beatson affair and, 82
  character assassination against, 82
  cloud of shame over, 82–83
  cult of, 263
  curiosity of, 28–29, 85
  as diplomat, 235
  first African expedition of, 49–55
  as hedonist, 25, 82–83
  illness of, 185–86
  infamous side of, 24–25
  journals of, 111
  languages spoken by, 25n
  lizard brain of, 105
  Mecca journey of, 24, 49–50

passion of, 124–25
prep for African trip by, 104
quitting of, 186–87
scar on cheek of, 86–87
Somaliland Expedition of, 25, 49, 86,
103–4, 106, 119
Speke's conflict with, 149–50, 216
Speke's debate with, 3–4
Speke's relationship with, 103–4, 110–11
syphilis of, 55
tomb of, 151
unconventional thinking of, 88
Burton-Speke Expedition, 107–11, 114–24,
148–49, 158–59, 181–82, 228, 268n
Burton's quitting on, 188–89
Burton's sickness on, 150, 152
daily ritual of, 111
finding of Tanganyika on, 153–54
malaria on, 149
Rusizi River in, 183–84
Speke's leaving of, 187–88
Speke's ophthalmia on, 152
timepiece broken in, 119–24
Burundi, 192
Byrd, Richard, 172

Cabot, Sebastian, 70n
Caesar, Julius, 78
Cain, Susan, 202
Cairo, 234
California, 30, 31
Cameron, Stanley, 153n
Cameron, Verney Lovett, 153n
camp followers, 110
Canada, 211
Canelos, 74
canned food, 169n
Cape of Good Hope, 91
Cape Town, 23, 37
caravan, 109–11
caravel (ship), 91–92, 102
Carlos IV, King of Spain, 176
Carnarvon, Earl of, 237–41, 244–45
death of, 245n–46n
Cartagena, 178
Carter, Howard, 241–45, 246
Casiquiare Canal, 177
Catherine the Great, 43–44, 45
Catholic Church, 61
Catholic missions, 30
caudate nucleus, 126

Central Slave and Ivory Trade Route, 109n
Chamonix, 137
Charlotte, Queen consort of England,
101n
Cherry-Garrard, Apsley, 9–10, 168
on Scott, 14
Chevalier, Pierre, 136
Chimborazo mountain, 179
cholera, 187
Christ, passion of, 125
Chuma, 147
Churchill, Winston, 97, 206, 234n, 237,
252
Church Missionary Society, 80–81
"Citizenship in a Republic" (Roosevelt),
191
Clark, William, 43, 211, 232
cloth, 184
cobras, 118
coffeehouses, 61n
Coleman, James, 128, 129
colonialism, 234
Columbus, Christopher, 15, 58, 60–61,
64–65, 71, 75, 92, 130n, 152, 176,
193–94, 201, 211
death of, 68
fourth voyage of, 63–64, 65–67
pessimism of, 71
third voyage of, 65
Commonwealth Trans-Antarctic
Expedition, 170n
Concorde, 201
concubines, 110
confidence, 224–25, 230
Congo bay owl, 192n
Congo River, 114, 115n
Conrad, Joseph, 93n
Conway, Rufus, 35
Cook, Frederick, 248
Cook, James, 29, 31, 32–34, 36, 39–41,
42, 45, 60, 62, 66, 70, 101n, 102,
128, 130n, 143, 155–56, 168, 175,
180n, 194, 201, 240, 246, 256
personal journals of, 43
statue of, 268, 268n
corporate culture, 165
courage, 14, 16–17, 104–5, 159–63, 172,
185
development of, 174–75
mediocrity as enemy of, 163–64
moral, 165–67, 173–74

INDEX

INDEX

INDEX

Johnson, Samuel, 38
Jones, Indiana (char.), 240
Jordan family, 20–21
Journal of Captain Cook's Last Voyage, A
  (Ledyard), 42

K2, 219
Kagera River, 192
Kama Sutra, 25
Kangchenjunga, 131
Karachi, 24–25, 184, 208
Kasumo, 192
Kazeh, 109, 149, 152, 155, 187, 188, 212
Kealakekua Bay, 33
Kensington Gardens, 266, 268
Kenya, Mount, 48–49
Kenya-Uganda Railway, 89n
Khartoum, 231–32
khat, 50
Kigoma, 158
Kilimanjaro, Mount, 48–49, 132
Kingani River, 124
King William Island, 93–95
Kirby, Mike, 13
Krapf, Johann, 48

Lachenal, Louis, 135, 136, 137
La Condamine, Charles Marie de, 72
La Perouse, Jean Françoise de, 40, 40n–41n
latitude, 120n
Laveran, Alphonse, 115n
Lawrence, T. E., 101, 164, 234n
lead poisoning, 170
Leakey, Louis, 247
learning goals, 63
Ledyard, John, 41–46
  aborted circumambulation of, 43–44,
  46
Leighton, Frederic, 86–87
leishmaniasis, 186
Leonardo da Vinci, 100–101
Lesseps, Ferdinand de, 214n
Lewis, C. S., 163
Lewis, Meriwether, 43, 211, 232
Libya, 157
Libyan Desert, 12
Lincoln, Abraham, 232–33
Lindbergh, Charles, 62–63, 206, 209
Lindsay, Martin, 226
Linnaean Association, 39
lions, 117

Livingstone, David, 7, 23, 62, 85, 143–48,
  181, 201, 236, 253, 256–57, 264–65,
  268
Livingstone, David (2011 medal winner),
  13
Livingstone, Mary, 143–44
lizard brain, 88–90, 95–96, 102, 105, 161
  as enemy of hope, 90–91
London, 6–7, 70–71, 187
London Geographical Society, 81
London School of Economics, 227n
longitude, 120, 121, 122, 123, 148–49
Louisiana Territory, 31
Louvre, 8
Lowther Lodge, 7–8
Lucas, Simon, 47
Luxor, 239–45

McKinley, Mount, 132, 248n
McKinley, William, 248n
Magdalena River, 178
Maizan, 218
malaria, 115–16, 115n, 123, 149
Mallory, George, 138, 139
mapmaking, 59, 120, 123
marine chronometers, 121–23, 127, 148–49
Maritime Geography and Statistics
  (Tuckey), 115n
Markham, Clements, 97–98, 97n
Mars, 29
mastery goals, 71
Matilda vipers, 118n
Matterhorn, 134
Maturin, Basil William, 225, 226
Maud, 142, 143n
Mazan, Lieutenant, 106
Mecca, 24, 49–50, 86, 184
mediocrity, 160–61, 163–64, 250
Mediterranean Ocean, 59
memory, 161, 200
Mercedes-Benz, 238n–39n
Meroe, 37
Meyer, Hans, 132n
"mindfulness," 229
Mississippi River, 77, 77n
Mont Analogue (Daumel), 270
Montesquieu, 79
moral courage, 165–67, 173–74
morality, 167
Morris, Jan, 141n
Moses, 78

INDEX

Imperial Trans-Antarctiv Expedition of, 96–97, 99–100
successful Antarctic expedition of, 98–99
Shepheard, Samuel, 234*n*
Shepheard Hotel, 234
Shipton, Eric, 140, 142*n*
Siberia, 44
Siberian fur trade, 44
Sikdhar, Radhanath, 131
Silurian System, The (Murchison), 84
Simpson, Thomas, 8
slavery, 64, 91, 108, 109
sleeping sickness, 116
Slocum, Joshua, 9
smallpox, 74
snakes, 117–19
Snow, Dr., 260–61
Snyder, Charles, 88
Sogdian Rock, 132
Somali coast, 49–50
Somaliland, 22–23, 24, 50, 51, 76
Somaliland Expedition, 25, 49, 86, 103–4, 105, 106, 119
somatic arousal, 161–63
South America, 65, 72, 175–76
Southern Ocean, 101
South Georgia Island, 101, 102, 103, 180*n*
South Pole, 12, 97, 99, 142, 167–74
space exploration, 210*n*, 247
Spain, 64, 69*n*, 73
Speke, John Hanning, 1–4, 10, 12, 18, 19–20, 22–23, 25–26, 49–50, 51, 52, 55–56, 59, 64, 76, 80, 87–88, 103, 104–5, 117, 146–47, 148, 166, 180–82, 194, 197–99, 201, 212–13, 214–15, 249, 252–53, 257, 260, 263, 266, 269
African knowledge of, 222
anger at Burton of, 111
Berbera attack on, 52–55
Burton's attempts to discredit, 213
Burton's conflict with, 149–50, 216
Burton's debate with, 3–4
Burton's invitation to join, 106
Burton's relationship with, 103–4, 110–11
characteristics of, 104
confidence of, 222
courage of, 104–5
curiosity of, 28–29
death of, 1, 259–61, 262–63
fall from grace of, 254–55

as hunter, 2, 21–22
illness of, 213
independence of, 199
in India, 21
intellect of, 236
journals of, 253–54
lack of fear in, 217–18
as loner, 20
monument of, 266–69
naïveté of, 22
Nile journey of, 216–17, 220–32
as ordinary, 20
as outsider, 22
passion of, 124–25
penchant for solitude of, 21
in return to England, 234–36
self-discipline of, 223–24, 228–29
source of Nile discovered by, 189–90, 195–97, 247
see also Burton-Speke Expedition
Speke, Mount, 180
Speke, William, 20
Speke-Grant expedition, 220–32
Speke Gulf, 180
Speke obelisk, 7
Speke's gazelle, 2, 180
Springsteen, Bruce, 17*n*
Stanley, Henry Morton, 62, 115*n*, 130, 145–46, 148*n*, 184, 201, 234*n*, 263, 265
Star Trek, 210*n*
State Department, U.S., 157, 158
Steinbauer, Wolfgang, 235*n*
Stockholm, 44
Stocks, J. Ellerton, 25
Stoddart, David, 11, 11*n*, 12
Stone Town Harbor, 107–8, 114
stress hormones, 161
stress response, 89
Stroyan, William, 49, 51–52, 54
Stuart, Andrew, 35
Stuart, Margaret, 115*n*
subgenual anterior cingulate cortex (sgACC), 162–63
Sudan, 31
Sudd, 79–80, 217
Suez Canal, 214*n*
sunglasses, 152
Superior, Lake, 197*n*
supplemental oxygen, 133
Susi, 147

INDEX

Swift, Jonathan, 166*n*
Sydney, Thomas Townshend, Viscount, 36
syphilis, 55

Tahiti, 31
Tana, Lake, 194*n*
Tanganyika, Lake, 109, 153–55, 158–59, 181, 185–86, 189, 197–98, 213, 261, 263, 265
  size of, 154*n*
Tanzania, 118, 158
Tanzanian National Railway, 201
Tarzan (Burroughs), 113
Tasmania, 92
Tennessee, 30–31
Terra Nova expedition, 167–74
Terray, Lionel, 135, 136, 137
Terror, 93, 94, 95, 98
Terror, Mount, 98
Thames River, 187
Theory of Intrinsic of Motivation, 16
"Three Jewels," 109
Tibet, 13
Timbuktu, 37, 47, 112
Times (London), 71, 227*n*
time zones, 122
Tinné, Alexandrine, 48
Tordesillas, Treaty of, 69
trabuco (gun), 30
travel writing, 59
Trinity College, 24
Truman, Harry, 227
Tsavo, 89–90
  man-eaters of, 89*n*–90*n*
tsetse flies, 116
Tuchman, Barbara, 61
Tuckey, James Hingston, 114–15, 115*n*, 148*n*
Tutankhamen, King, 245, 246
20,000 Leagues Under the Sea (Verne), 93*n*
typhoid, 177

Ujiji, 87, 104, 109, 145, 150, 151, 152, 155–56, 158–59, 183, 184, 186, 265
United States, 77
  westward expansion of, 210–11

Valley of the Kings, 241–45, 246*n*
Varthema, Ludovico di, 26

ventromedial prefrontal cortex, 250
Verbiest, Ferdinant, 238*n*
Verne, Jules, 93*n*
Vespucci, Amerigo, 68
Victoria, Lake, 196–99, 212, 213, 220, 230, 261, 263, 265
  size of, 197
  Speke's map of, 215
  waterfall at, 230–31
Victoria, Queen of England, 28, 84, 112, 130, 144, 268*n*
Victoria Falls, 113
Victorian era of African exploration, 111–12
Vikings, 168
vitriolic acid, 46
Voyage of Saint Brendan the Abbot, The, 60, 61

Waldecker, Burkhardt, 192
Walpole, Horace, 38
Watt, Eddie, 128
Watt, Gertrude, 128, 130
Waugh, Andrew, 130–31
Wellington, Duke of, 21
White Nile, 194
Whymper, Edward, 134
Wilderness Road, 31
Will and the Ways, The (Snyder), 88
William III, King of England (William of Orange), 70
William IV, King of England, 8, 11, 81, 93
Wilson, Edward, 98, 173, 174
Winter Palace Hotel, 240
Witkin, Herman, 199–200
World War I, 97, 244
World War II, 139
Wright, Orville and Wilbur, 205
Wright, Thomas, 82–83
wristwatches, 121*n*
writer's block, 89

Yangtze River, 77*n*
Yeager, Chuck, 223–24
Younghusband, Francis, 26–27, 246
  in walk from Peking to Bombay, 27

Zambezi River, 23, 144, 181, 256–57, 265
Zanzibar, 107–8, 114, 115, 214, 216

ABOUT THE AUTHOR

Martin Dugard is the *New York Times* bestselling author of *Into Africa*, *The Training Ground*, and *Last Voyage of Columbus*. He is also the co-author, with political commentator Bill O'Reilly, of *Killing Lincoln*, *Killing Kennedy*, and *Killing Jesus*; and with James Patterson, *The Murder of King Tut*. Dugard was the executive producer and writer of *A Warrior's Heart*, a feature film released in December 2011. He lives in Southern California.

Dugard, Martin.

The explorers.

$26.00